Gary Sinclair

# Never Quit Climbing

## *Overcoming Life's Seemingly Insurmountable Mountains*

Printed in the United States

ISBN: 9781790797226

Published by Never Quit Climbing
Indianapolis, Indiana in conjunction with
KDP/Amazon

www.neverquitclimbing.com

Cover design by Amy Tripple,
www.twelvestonesphotography.com

To my favorite climbers – my wife Jackie, son Tim Sinclair and daughter Amy Tripple plus all those brave and caring enough to climb with us, whether high on a mountain or alongside on our cancer journey. I love you all.

# Table of Contents

# Climb On!

# INTRODUCTION

*"Never measure the height of a mountain until you have reached the top. Then you will see how low it was."*

***Dag Hammarskjold***

I first fell in love with mountains as a young boy. With very limited means, my parents, Harold and Beverly Sinclair, scraped up enough money for several adventurous vacations out west for my sister Marilyn and me. My dad loved planning the routes and researching interesting stops along the way. Mom worked out plans for food and other needs we might encounter. How they both would have loved today's power of the Internet to dig deeper into the details!

During several summers we departed our little home in Michigan and drove thousands of miles to places like the Grand Tetons, Glacier National Park and the Rockies.

On the earliest trips we camped in a huge canvas tent that slept six. It took an hour or more just to set the monstrosity up. We had to unfold it, lay it out on the grass, hammer the huge poles and stakes into the ground and finally hoist everything into a standing position. If we had camped in the rain on an earlier night the whole campsite smelled like dirty laundry.

Rickety old cots and sleeping bags were eventually added inside. Finally, we unpacked the camp stove, lantern, lawn chairs and coolers to round out our home for the night.

A few years later my grandma and grandpa purchased a sixteen-foot travel trailer that we pulled behind one of the cars, usually a large Pontiac. Our new rolling motel, a metal box on wheels, served us well on several more vacations to the high country.

In fact, six of us, four adults and two children, slept in our upscale digs every night for as long as two weeks. To this day I'm not sure how that worked! It's probably best not to remember.

Nevertheless, we didn't obsess over our lack of personal amenities. We knew that serious, experienced travelers owned much better equipment than we had but we didn't care. We were headed to the mountains! In fact, at least twice we returned to Wyoming and Colorado for a second round of altitude rather than travel to a non-mountainous location!

When I was in high school mom and dad added an amazing first visit to *Yosemite National Park* in California. This majestic valley contains some of the most stunning cliffs and peaks in the world. Unfortunately, we faced a tough time getting there as our car broke down in the middle of Iowa the second day out. Several nights were spent living out of the trailer while parked in the side lot of a truck stop. But thanks to an amazing mechanic and our commitment to keep going we still made it.

But one of those mountain experiences changed everything for me. When I was eleven and very excited about another excursion to Colorado my mom, dad and I agreed to ascend *Long's Peak* with one of my grandma's friends. He was an experienced climber who'd tackled and summited *Long's* numerous times and agreed to accompany us on our ascent.

Every fourteen thousand foot mountain presents a challenge but *Long's* is one of the tougher ones. Even its simplest route demands a lot from the average climber. Each participant must overcome several levels of difficulty and physical demands to reach the summit.

In addition, the trailhead to the top and back totals sixteen miles, including a relentlessly steep trail, thousands of boulders, snow, dangerous ledges and an imposing *Home Stretch*. Nonetheless, with our competent guide to lead us, we were confident of our ability to get to the top.

Our self-assurance quickly deteriorated.

Upon reaching *Boulder Field,* a very apt moniker for a relentless section of climbing at thirteen thousand feet, my dad and I were forced to quit because of extreme mountain sickness. Before long, after several bouts of vomiting and the dizziness that often plagues lowlanders at high elevations, the two of us were headed back down the mountain. Amazingly my mom continued on to the top with the initial group climbing what is known today as the old cables route.

In contrast, I was devastated by not having finished. I vowed before we ever reached the car that someday I would return to the scene of my failure and complete the climb no matter what.

Thirty years later my then thirteen-year-old son Tim and I gutted our way through *Boulder Field* without any nausea and courageously made our way up the rest of the mountain. We almost stopped at one point when we heard scary news about the infamous *ledges* but continued anyway notching our first *fourteener*. What a thrill it was to finally succeed and better yet get there with my son!

Since then I've summited eight other fourteeners, several with Tim, three with my daughter Amy, one with a friend and one with Jackie. (More on that later.)

Though I didn't know it at the time I was learning and would eventually embrace a powerful truth, one that years later would take on significant, personal meaning. Here it is:

*Overcoming mountains of granite has much to teach us about defeating our personal ones*!

We all have private mountains. Everyone has a high places story. You do. I do. There are hundreds of origins of course. The most obvious rise up out of poor health, broken relationships, financial challenges, job difficulties, addictions and the loss of loved ones. But no matter the category or cause, the challenge to overcome them can seem well . . . mountainous at best.

They often cast an ominous shadow on our comfortable life and breed big-time worry like an *Everest, Denali, Kilimanjaro or The Matterhorn* would for the novice climber. They require going to places we've never been before. We can't imagine how we're going to overcome them and wonder if we could face anything worse.

We may even find ourselves living with a panic that robs our sleep, races our heart and confounds our mind. If you already identify with a comparable overwhelming dread you're not alone. The apprehension by itself can be a game stopper, a huge weight that we carry with us everywhere we go if we hang on to it.

But as we'll learn together, our emotions can be managed and used to guide us on our difficult, even dangerous journey. When paired with courage, our negative emotions can become as asset. I'll talk later about how to use our anxiety, even dread to lead to success.

Mark Twain once said, *"Courage is resistance to fear – mastery of fear, not the absence of fear." (Pudd'nhead Wilson's Calendar)*

In *Never Quit Climbing* I'll share several key concepts that will give you more courage to battle your personal mountains. Each idea is extremely practical and can be applied to even the toughest climbs.

I'll also tell how Jackie and I had to overcome our biggest mountain, one that serves as a model for how to incorporate these concepts and principles into daily life.

The good news is that you don't have to have climbed your own peak in the Rockies, Alps or Himalayas to use these concepts. You might find the principles more vivid and *rock solid* (excuse the pun) by having a physical summit under your belt but that's not mandatory.

Even if the closest you've come to a mountain is seeing *Mount Rushmore* or visiting *Mount Holyoke*, you can become a better life climber now or in the future. In time you can begin to scale personal heights with new confidence, hope and determination.

Learning the ropes (oops another one) will take time and perseverance. On a high-altitude mountain you quickly discover breathing becomes harder and harder the higher you go. The strain will get worse before it improves. Your muscles work harder while the stress of the elevation can play mind games, casting doubt on your ability to summit. I can't tell you how many times I've literally said to myself, "*Never quit climbing, Gary.*"

The main goal in the chapters that follow is to teach you how to *keep going* when your personal trail gets steeper, the air thinner, the pain greater and the desire to quit overwhelming. The urge to stop can be relentless.

Like runners in a marathon race, climbers face walls of pain, exhaustion and discouragement that can bring them to a screeching halt long before they've finished. You'll learn how to run or walk through and beyond the walls of your expedition that threaten to stop you. I'll also cover the essentials to bring with you, items that can provide additional resources for strength when you need it.

Facing your personal mountain will not be easy. It never is. Most of the world's biggest mountains are extremely dangerous. *The Matterhorn* claimed five hundred lives in just over a century of climbing. It wasn't until the 1950's that *Everest* was finally topped. Just recently I saw online that two more climbers died during the best climbing season.

The good news is that there are hundreds of peaks that were once thought impossible to scale that have now been conquered. Similarly, there are myriad stories of life overcomers who have reached their goal and completed their quest because they didn't quit.

Much of your resolve to summit must reside within the core of your being, your soul. That kind of determination has to be in place before you ever start from the trailhead to and serve as the underpinning of your commitment to make it.

That day on *Long's Peak* with Tim was unforgettable and fulfilling in so many ways. However, there were many times when we were both ready to turn around. Thankfully I remembered back to age eleven when I said to myself, *"Gary, you will someday defeat this mountain."* I still possessed my commitment from dozens of years earlier.

You have to do the same. Put a line in the sand now. Step across it and before reading any more of this book promise yourself that you will *never quit climbing* up the mountain ahead of you.

Of course, I'll talk about various versions of success and what they may mean, require or force you to accept. There are times on mountains when you do have to turn back. That happens and misguided resolve in those circumstances can be deadly. Nevertheless, the drive to keep going in the right conditions is imperative for summiting.

Are you ready to start your climb? Are you fired up to take on your mountain or continue the climb you've already begun? I hope so. The view from the top is worth it. So, let's get going. Climb on.

# Part I:
## We Just Can't Avoid Mountains

# CHAPTER 1: WHY WE NEED MOUNTAINS

*"The good Lord gave us mountains so we could learn how to climb."*
*From the song, Mountains, by* **Lonestar**.

Jackie and I have been fortunate to travel to numerous picturesque mountain ranges in the United States, Canada, Asia and Europe. We've hiked in the Swiss and Austrian Alps, Yosemite Valley, Denali National Park, the Canadian Rockies, Great Smokey Mountains and of course the Colorado Rockies.

We've trekked up to and onto the Great Wall of China. It surprised us that many sections rest on the spine of low altitude mountain ranges. Just getting to the wall is quite a hike in itself! As a result, I was able to zoom down a zip line from the wall to lower elevation, gliding hundreds of feet above a gorgeous lake. How cool is that!!

Jackie and I have never tired discovering new snow-capped ranges, sheer granite walls or sunlit peaks wherever they are. There is something wonderfully calming about rambling along a trail in near silence with the only sounds being our boots hitting the ground, a bird chirping or a soft breeze blowing.

We typically start our hikes before sunrise to avoid storms that can erupt on summits after noon. Our early starts sometimes warrant watching the sun come up on nearby peaks, awakening our day as it paints nearby ranges with brilliant color. We may also observe wildlife finishing their nightlong jaunts or beginning their day.

In fact, most of our mountain memories are drenched with unforgettable awe, wonder, beauty, surprise and the fulfillment of long held dreams and bucket list entries.

I distinctly remember our trip to Austria and Switzerland celebrating our twenty-fifth wedding anniversary. We of course included the *Sound of Music* tour in Austria and enjoyed trekking (as they like to call it over there) in and around the surrounding villages. We stayed in a small lake town not too far from Salzburg which served as home base for most of our excursions.

Jackie still remembers her embarrassment filming me in a lovely white apron spinning around in a field like Julie Andrews. I made sure, too, that the Alps were prominent in the background. A friend later added music to the video. It was a classic (and rather hilarious) moment for sure!

But one of our major reasons for going to that part of the world was to see *The Matterhorn* in Switzerland. As a kid I over and over read a book entitled *Banner in the Sky* by James Ramsey Ullman. It's the story of a young boy who loved to climb and dreamed of being one of the first to conquer the area's biggest, most challenging unclimbed peak.

While not called *The Matterhorn* in the book, Ullman clearly wrote his work with this glorious peak in mind. A Hollywood movie was produced years later called *Third Man on the Mountain* affirming that premise. Nonetheless, I found myself imagining the day when I could actually stand in its presence gazing at this gem of the Alps. It was one thing as a child to read about it but another to see it as an adult.

We stayed in a little apartment for five days in the quaint, very Swiss hamlet of Zermatt, blessed with rare bright sunshine and blue sky the entire time. Each day we relished breathtaking views of this storied mountain both from panoramic distances or by hiking in nearby valleys and saddles.

Thousands of visitors from all over the world arrive on the train each day to take pictures of this wondrous needle proudly pointing skyward. Words are insufficient to describe its sheer beauty and size while serving as the centerpiece for a seemingly unending array of other peaks. At times we wondered if we had died and gone to Heaven!

One day Jackie and I agreed that I could attempt a solo hike to get somewhat closer. Okay, I talked her into it since, don't forget, this was our anniversary trip. I so wanted to hike to the highest point of *The Matterhorn* reachable that time of year. It was an extremely steep, long hike and challenge so I would do it alone and be very careful in the process.

The next morning, I got up early and started the trail that most technical climbers utilize for their summit bid during season. For several hours I meandered through herds of sheep and cattle grazing in the high grasses. There were surprisingly few other hikers to be seen that time of year. Soon I spotted the tree line and knew I was getting closer to my goal.

Up to that point I was shielded from the actual *Matterhorn* even to sneak a brief glimpse. And while I enjoyed the magnificence of nearby peaks worthy of their own acclaim, I could think of little else besides seeing the mountain I had so dreamed about!

Soon I approached what would be the last switchback. It certainly seemed like at least the hundredth that day. As my eyes rose above the final mound of grass and rock, my heart skipped a beat and then I saw it. I came face to face with *The Matterhorn* itself, glorious, snow-covered, a heavenly prism sparkling brightly in a cloudless sky. I'd made it!

Emotion flooded my soul as tears welled up in my eyes. I felt small while in the presence of something magnificent. Instead of seeing it far off in the distance it now rose nearly straight above me. It was a holy moment surrounded by a divine beauty that I will never forget.

Jackie and I have sensed similar emotional stirrings everywhere there are mountains. The high peaks, with their jagged ruggedness, sparkling snow and stunning strength, reflect a splendor that words simply can't chronicle.

Mountains hold a rare intrigue, mystery and grandeur that have a way of unearthing inner, deep longings and passions, many that we never knew we had. Perhaps some of their impact resides in their being void of noise, pace and demands that everyday life at home seems to require.

We need mountains, if for no other reason, to help us regroup, retool and re-think about why we're here, what's important and how we're going to live out the rest of our days. Mountains like *The Matterhorn* are magnificent in so many ways and to be enjoyed.

But mountains are also rugged, rocky, unpredictable and far bigger when you stand next to them or begin to climb one.

Our personal challenges, the mountains we are experiencing now or will encounter someday, will also be tougher to conquer than we imagined. But we still need their benefits in spite of the risks and corresponding hardships.

First though there are some risks.

## The Dangers on a Mountain

Sheer cliffs, fierce storms, violent winds, destructive avalanches and a host of other hazards like falling rocks, wild animals, accidents, etc. require that we treat mountains wisely and respectfully. The dangers in the high places don't care about age, reputation, skill or heritage. They will take you or me out if we're not careful.

*Mountains can kill you.*

Nearly three hundred people have died trying to climb *Everest* over the years. People die on *Long's Peak* every year, often from lightning and other bad weather that can erupt out of nowhere.

One of the most poignant segments of our trip to *The Matterhorn* was strolling through a cemetery in town reading the names of climbers who were killed attempting to summit this beautiful, but deadly citadel.

Your personal climbs can also lead to disaster. You can get sideswiped by unexpected outcomes or difficulties just as one would above tree line. Emotions can flare up under the new pressures. When life's mountains suddenly appear your first response may be anger or at best a questioning of why you need to climb this peak in the first place.

You might wonder, *"Why must I endure this difficulty? Who's going to solve all the unknowns I'm facing right now? This is too big for me to handle!"* As a result, you can become paralyzed by fear. *Fear* can cause you to run the other way, to seek out the flat land and return to life the way you've always known it. Fear can lead to impulsiveness and taking unnecessary or unwise chances.

If you're a person of faith, you might become mad at God, chastising the Creator for allowing you to undergo these mountain-sized challenges that appear to be more than you can handle.

You might literally agonize as some do claiming from God a healing, provision or a better answer. The result essentially leads to a demand that God get rid of your mountain instead of having to beat it.

You might choose to believe that if you just pray more, read the Bible more, fast more, eat a different diet, lead a simpler life, join a small group or give more to charity that God is obligated to at least ease up on your problems.

Isn't there a better way to grow than having to conquer an *Everest*? *"Can't God turn my Himalayan peak into a Smokey Mountains' one?* we wonder.

And the answer is often, "*No*," Many times there isn't a better answer at least from God's point of view or in the general scheme of life. You may still have to summit a peak that seems impossible to overcome. But there are reasons, good, even life-altering causes for why a mountain may be in your life for a while.

*Mountains can be relentless*

Even on the best of days, most big mountains are just that: BIG. The trails go on and on, up and up. It's rare that you can climb a high peak in less than two-thirds of a day and many times it takes far longer.

There are scores of switchbacks, boulders to overcome and thin air that makes breathing far more challenging. The possibility of a storm in the Rockies after noon is a regular threat and something climbers prepare for by starting early, usually before dawn .

Most of the routes I've done on 14000 foot mountains were at least 8-10 miles round trip, the first half largely being up.

Our personal mountains can be relentless too. We think the challenge will never be over. The days get long, tedious and boring. But a time can come when you'll really be better if you'll keep heading toward your summit.

I'll give some hints later on how to do that well..

*Mountains can be deceiving*

Sometimes you can think that a peak you've decided to tackle isn't that bad. Don't believe it. The easy trail that seems like no big deal can all of a sudden become a skating rink.

Rain might start pelting the shale, the trail can suddenly deteriorate causing you to bushwhack back to somewhere familiar or a snow storm rolls in from out of nowhere.

Never take a mountain lightly. Prepare, read what you can, keep looking ahead for possible danger spots. Don't take unnecessary risks like going off the trail or considering a shortcut that looks better and easier.

Mountain rock that looks safe from a distance can become a death trap because you face unexpected difficulty moving up or down. If a mountain has been deemed especially difficult, think about getting a guide to lead the way. I'll talk about climbing with other people in an upcoming chapter.

For now, let me simply say, *Don't fear your personal mountain, but respect it every step of the way.*

## REASONS TO WELCOME HIGH ALTITUDE

We live in a culture where more and more people want things to be *instant* and *now*. But in reality, overcoming a mountain, any kind of mountain, granite or personal, is rarely a quick process. Let me suggest some reasons why that's a good thing.

*Great results usually require extraordinary efforts.*

There are few monumental achievements that don't cost something. They can require *money, time, a limit to friendships, pain, loss of social status and decreased comfort.*

The Olympics are one of my favorite sporting events. I love to see the amazing talents, results, accomplishments and stories that color every athlete's journey. Their experience on the world stage every four years is usually life changing and one they (and in many cases *we)* will never forget.

However, we dare not ignore the extreme sacrifices they made to get there. Becoming a world-class athlete is a status few achieve and remains extremely hard and very competitive. Only a percentage of those who do all the training actually make it to the big event.

In one of the last competitions a fifteen-year-old won a gold medal in figure skating! Similarly, a seventeen-year-old girl took the gold in snowboarding. How much of their lives do you suppose was committed to achieving those amazing awards? *Most of it.*

Think of some of the most talented people you know, famous or not. How did they become a surgeon, lawyer, world-class musician, scholar, orator, acclaimed writer or super athlete?

They had to commit a huge chunk of their waking life to being the best and it cost them dearly. To use my vernacular, they climbed a host of personal mountains to reach the top. Some of them faced trails littered with injuries, financial ruin, relationship disasters, countless moves and even abuse.

But those tests made them stronger, more determined and tougher so that they could face the pressures an Olympic run requires. Their *mountains* developed courage, character and competencies that will prepare them for life beyond their athletic victories.

Often after major victories, athletes will tell a probing television or news reporter that their win proved that *if you can dream it you can do it.* Nothing could be further from reality. *Dreams don't get people to their summits. Commitment and hard work do.* You have to know how to get to the top and then do it!

I've said to my kids and spouse each time we've climbed a new trail that only a fraction of a percent of the world's population has stood where we've stood. Few have eaten a sack lunch in the beautiful locations we've been privileged to enjoy.

Why? Because few are willing to pay the high price of getting to the top of a mountain or at least above the tree line. Few are excited enough to get up early, face steep trails, stop every twenty steps because of the altitude and hike as much as eight to fifteen miles in a day to reach the summit and get back down.

It's always easier to look at mountaintops from a distance. It's very unlikely that we'll become all we could be if we don't have a few mountains to climb, if we're never pushed beyond our normal limits. Mountains compel us to go higher than we've ever gone before.

High altitude climber extraordinaire, Ed Viesturs, has conquered the fourteen tallest peaks in the world at least once, all without supplemental oxygen.

In many ways he seems superhuman and he does have certain physical capacities that the average person doesn't enjoy. But in his book, *No Shortcuts To The Top,* which outlines Viesturs' treks on each summit, he says this,

> *"There is nothing else in life like getting to the summit. What's more, I've always felt that the greater the challenge, the greater the reward."*

Of course, as I said in the *Introduction*, we don't have to climb physical mountains to be stretched and grow. But personal mountains, like the real thing, mature us and result in long-lasting, impactful results deep within. We attain outcomes that would never bear fruit without these high-altitude *challenges* in our lives.

*Elevation helps us see with greater perspective.*

Read any book on *Mt. Everest* and you'll hear the phrase from successful climbers that they were, *"On top of the world."* And in one sense they're right. There is no other place on earth that looks down on everything else like standing at 29,000 plus feet. You can't go any higher!

However, you don't have to climb *Everest* to enjoy a top of the world experience. *Long's Peak* is the highest point in *Rocky Mountain National Park* and the view from the summit is gorgeous. There too you can feel like you're on top of the world, at least a part of it.

Looking east there are the vast plains beyond the city of Denver. To the west are multiple summits, a significant percentage of the fifty-four peaks over fourteen thousand feet in Colorado alone. It's all a part of a 360-degree panorama few ever see. To me it produces a holy, awe-inducing, spectacular encounter with this planet on which we reside.

There are sights we would never see at lower altitudes. Little lakes, hidden by surrounding peaks and granite walls, suddenly come into view, dotting the mountain landscape with bright specks of color.

Animals who roam above tree line can be spotted in their natural habitats far above the valley below. Even the clouds and the potential storms they may form appear loftier, brighter and more menacing at times.

We may learn things about life and our part in it. For example, the busyness of our personal world is laid aside for a time. In those moments, we can become aware again of how jam-packed our schedule is these days. I know that I have often, in the stillness of the thin air, recalled how rarely I stop to ponder the extraordinary realities all around me.

I have remembered that I had not slowed much recently to enjoy the laugh of a grandson, the maturity of my grown kids, the beauty of my wife or the myriad ways we have been blessed with possessions and comforts.

It's on the high ground that we will gain new or renewed appreciation for creation, its bigness, smallness, grandeur and beauty. Personal mountains help us better appreciate what really matters. They show us again that *we are not alone in this life* either in general or while tackling our unique struggles.

As I alluded to earlier, one of the perks of climbing is the natural camaraderie that fellow hikers enjoy. We take time to talk, tell stories and share our resources like water, candy bars or energy food. People often emerge in our everyday lives who are also climbing their own mountain. It's on the trail that we often realize how many others are climbing concurrently with us.

Climbing can remind us that we do not need to make our journeys alone. Often our difficult expedition connects us to others we never saw coming who actually care about us and our climb because they have been on the trail too.

I remember on that first *Long's Peak* venture a group of hikers eventually passed Tim and I well above tree line. But as they overtook us, I noticed that one twenty–something woman was lagging behind, struggling to keep up.

In fact, we soon saw that the other two hikers, both guys, unapologetically moved ahead at a quicker pace leaving the young lady to fend for herself.

Within a few minutes she looked back and asked if she could hike with us for a while. We said, "*Of course*," and she joined Tim and me all the way to the summit.

While I was pretty gassed for the remainder of the hike (Tim was like a mountain goat), I also remember being somewhat energized because we now had to think about someone else. We later celebrated together at the top some 14, 255 feet above sea level.

*Mountains strengthen us for future situations*

I will never forget a comment my son made not too long after our *Long's Peak* climb. Tim was an avid basketball player and had started his fall workouts for the upcoming season.

He came home one day, however, and after a particularly tough practice said,

> *"You know, dad, sometimes when we're running wind sprints and I wonder if I can make it, I remember that I climbed Long's Peak!"*

By overcoming one mountain he realized that he could tackle another. That's worth something, isn't it? In fact, now pretty late in life, I reflect on my successes and remind myself that even though I'm getting older, I'm not about to quit. I've climbed 14er's and 13er's even in the past few years and the view from the top is still worth it!

Those accomplishments give me hope and inspiration that I can do something big again even if it takes a little (ok, a lot) longer!

And while it's important to prepare well for a high-altitude adventure, a good amount of extra conditioning occurs during the climb.

In fact, for the average person and those of us who regularly live at lower elevations it's very difficult to prepare for the debilitating effects of altitude.

If you're wise, when you get to your destination you spend as many days as possible acclimatizing to the new surroundings, working out at varying altitudes days before your ascent.

Climbers in the Himalayas, for example, who will be heading to what is called *The Death Zone* above 26,000 feet, literally spend weeks and months adjusting to the thinner air even if they plan to use supplemental oxygen.

Because there are so many unplanned things that can go wrong on any mountain, becoming stronger and learning to react quickly and correctly must be practiced over and above one's pre-trip preparation. Some of that can only occur on the climb itself.

Tim and I were climbing another 14er called *Mount of the Holy Cross.* It too is a demanding climb in part because during the ascent hikers must still descend over a thousand vertical feet. That means on the hike back when everyone is exhausted you have to re-climb that thousand vertical feet!

And for you non-hikers one thousand vertical feet doesn't mean merely covering a thousand feet of trail. No, it requires switch-backing many times until you have climbed a thousand feet *vertically*! Given that *Holy Cross* includes another boulder-laden, route finding, sketchy trail push to the summit, the additional climb on the return trip is a gut buster for the average person.

Unfortunately, Tim and I got somewhat lost coming down because we were not as careful as we should have been about setting up *cairns,* piles of rock, that would mark our return trip. They help guide the way through a field of boulders that all looks the same especially from above.

After some time trying to get lower on the mountain to outrun a storm, traversing a snow field and stumbling upon a trail, we amazingly discovered we were on the right path and made it back down. (I'll come back to that experience later in another context.)

We learned an important lesson about navigation during our scary descent, thankful to have found our way. We couldn't have practiced that somewhere else. We're stronger hikers and tougher people because we faced this extra challenging peak. Mountains have a way of doing that.

*Mountains prepare us to help others*

Lastly, mountains in life are the foundation stones for guiding others up similar pathways. To truly emphasize this point and set the stage for many of the principles to follow I need to tell you more of our story.

### OUR PERSONAL MOUNTAIN

As I mentioned in the last chapter, I've climbed nine fourteeners and a few thirteeners over the years. But one of the later summit bids I made included Jackie. She loves to hike, has often trekked well above tree line but until a decade and a half ago had never stood on top of a fourteener.

However, on this particular trip without any kids or friends along, I suggested I would be trying another summit on my own. Yes, I know you're not supposed to climb alone but I was planning a route that I knew would be filled with other hikers. I wouldn't technically be by myself, right? *(No emails or letters please.)*

So, Jackie asked if I thought she could do this one with me. *Grey's Peak* wasn't that tough of a climb compared to many so I responded, *"Of course, why not? If we don't make it, no big deal. I won't leave you there by yourself."*

As always, we got an early start, made our way up a treacherous road to the trailhead and began our climb while the sun was rising. It was a beautiful day and the trail was filled with the usual rocks under every step (that's why these mountains are called *The Rockies*).

Thankfully the altitude change was gradual for a while. However, as we got closer to our goal there were scores of relentless switchbacks leading us up a climbers' trail.

We eventually made it, though not without the usual pain and labored breathing high altitude can produce. It was especially tough going for Jackie as she seemed pretty peeked and worn out when we summited. But, hey, it's always harder at the top, right?

As the snow flurries started, we stepped onto the summit of *Gray's Peak*. We celebrated, enjoyed our victory for several minutes and took a few pictures. We then began our descent sooner than usual since storms aren't generally predictable in Colorado and the summit is the last place to be in a storm.

The trip down was shorter of course and Jackie seemed to feel much better heading back. We celebrated again that night with a delicious dinner followed by a lengthy soaking in the hot tub at the condo.

Three months later Jackie went to a routine appointment with a specialist at the urging of our regular doctor. He said her minor symptoms were really nothing to worry about but wanted to be extra cautious and totally sure something more serious had been ruled out.

In fact, because of the apparently normal nature of this appointment I didn't go with them. Instead I encouraged our daughter Amy to accompany her mom and spend some time together afterwards.

Unfortunately, it wasn't long before Jackie called me and said that the specialist was convinced that she had stage three-colon/rectal cancer. Shocked? Of course. We obviously never saw that coming. We immediately knew we had another mountain to climb!

That day was the beginning of eighteen months of tests, doctor visits, chemo, radiation and surgeries. It was a huge mountain, one from which we would learn much through many hardships and challenges we would have rather done without.

We immediately asked lots of tough questions:

> "*Why her? Had they missed the tumor (apparently they had)? Will she die? Where do we start? Where will we go from here?* "

This was new territory for us so the only thing we knew to do was find out more.

What I'm sharing in this book is largely a result of what happened next and what life and our faith taught us during those succeeding eighteen months. I can tell you before we head deeper into the story that Jackie is doing well today with only minor inconveniences and symptoms remaining. The cancer itself is gone.

However, we have had the honor and privilege since then of using Jackie's cancer experience combined with years of treks in high places to assist others on their difficult climbs. Our unexpected crucible made us much more reliable and trustworthy to be of help even though our peaks may be different than theirs. We're hoping our story and lessons learned will help you too!

I'll tell more of our story throughout the rest of the book, how we made it and the implications for you. But for now, don't forget that your mountain experience can become an incredibly powerful platform and source of strength for others who may follow behind you.

On a different trip to Colorado, Jackie and I were hiking what was supposed to be a somewhat recreational trail to a beautiful mountain lake. Unfortunately, early on we experienced huge, biting flies, a steep, but overgrown trail, lousy scenery and most importantly no sign of a lake.

We soon found ourselves thinking that we would turn around so I suggested that Jackie wait at one of the few shady spots we'd come upon. Before we gave up, I would hike ahead to see if we might actually be closer to the lake than we thought.

I started up the still steep incline wondering if the additional time we would spend was even worth it. To my surprise in a half mile or so I came to the lake! It was actually quite beautiful! I hurried back down the trail to where Jackie was waiting and explained that she could definitely make it. Continuing the journey would be worth the effort. While I couldn't take the hard climb away I could encourage her that she too could make it.

That's what we do when we have pre-climbed part of someone's trail. We walk alongside to let them know they can make it, to give *hope* when it seems distant or gone. Our having already been up the trail can provide that needed last bit of incentive and inspiration to get someone else to the summit.

If you're still overwhelmed by a mountain or two looming over you right now, take a moment to think about, talk about and even anticipate what good outcomes might await you as you face the high country of life.

Is it possible that God will take you to new heights that you will someday thank Him for, even though the journey was especially tough? I can tell you from experience that the climb will be worth it. Hard? Probably. But remember, most good things are.

*Things To Think About In Chapter 1*

What scares me the most about my mountain? What's the worst thing that could happen?

What are some of the unknowns that are making this climb seem difficult?

What things tend to make me want to not even start my climb? Is there anything I can do to reduce those?

# CHAPTER 2: FACING YOUR MOUNTAINS HONESTLY

*"There is nothing so strong or safe in an emergency of life as the simple truth."* **Charles Dickens**

Sometimes life stinks, doesn't it? We think a smooth path is ahead for a while but then bad things happen or people disappoint us and our life gets harder again. From out of nowhere, a troublesome event, person or circumstance bursts onto our personal scene and an easy journey turns into a nightmare or at best a major storm.

When Jackie and I planned to have our second child, we believed that three years between kids would be perfect until it was discovered Jackie had endometriosis. Months of tests and trying to conceive stretched the timeframe two more years. Other times we received extra money as a gift only to have an emergency come along that drained away most of our additional resources.

Most of us draw up big plans, dream special dreams, get excited about inspiring opportunities and eagerly adopt new roles that can quickly become overwhelming or turn in negative directions. Unplanned bombshells explode or throw unexpected roadblocks before us that we didn't see coming. A mountain enters our world.

These adversities arise from multiple origins including ones we brought on ourselves. We ate too much, screwed up at work, flunked out of school, made wrong choices or destroyed a good relationship. Our *Mt. Everest* may be partly our fault.

If so, we can beat ourselves up and feel paralyzed believing we're unable to do anything about our problems. We're ashamed, embarrassed and argue that our predicament is a penalty from life or even God for messing up in the first place.

Other challenges, however, were not our doing. Doctors discovered cancer, our company down-sized, a family member went off the reservation, age caught up with us, someone we love was killed by a drunk driver or an accident sent us to rehab. And we now know that a worldwide pandemic can rearrange everyone's plans.

In these situations, we can respond with a wide range of emotion. We get angry, panicky or depressed and tempted to give up. Personal progress is stymied but for different reasons. Instead we start asking "Why?" believing that something or someone in this world doesn't like us. We get mad at God or whoever and demand answers because we think life should have kept us from the struggle.

Unfortunately, neither response fosters effective and restorative progress. Both tend to stop us in our tracks rather than motivate us to move forward, get to higher ground and overcome. We need to ask, "*How?*" but still focus on "*How come?*"

That's why we need to accept our mountains including their lurking steep trails, sheer cliffs and other dangers. Until we look those challenges in the eye, admit they are significant and determine to overcome them, we'll wait, stall or never even start the journey to defeat them.

In spite of the classic response for decades from climbers who said they conquer mountains merely because they are there, mountains serve a far greater, more important purpose than to just be conquered or bagged for one's bucket list.

The common climber mantra sounds a bit philosophical, esoteric, and even romantic in a way but it's really not accurate. People make their way to mountaintops for many other reasons. Some seek a sense of *accomplishment.* They have proving to do to themselves or others. That was me on *Long's Peak.*

For a smaller group their goals may be more pragmatic: to stay in shape, spend time with friends or outdo their personal best. What you will rarely hear from those who head for the high country is, "*I climb mountains because they are easy.*"

Mountain climbing is hard.

That's part of the intrigue, the challenge and the lure. It's not just because the mountain is there. People climb because there's something bigger than themselves to defeat. The details may vary, but seasoned climbers learn to embrace each mountain for what it is rather than pretend it's easy or not there in the first place.

Serious climbers spend days, weeks, even months preparing. They learn the routes, pitfalls, hazards and options they will face. They read about or listen to the stories of those who have climbed before them. They accept the resultant fears and do what they can to lessen them.

So where should we start if we're going to be totally candid, avoid running from our mountains and instead overcome them?

## Honesty Is The Best Policy

Hundreds of climbers each year are willing to spend sixty to a hundred thousand dollars to have a guide take them to the summit of *Mt. Everest* or a similar Himalayan peak.

Most of the high adventure companies and their guides are upstanding, honest business and mountaineering people. A few unfortunately accept climbers who should never be attempting mountains of that magnitude no matter how much money they have.

These typically novice or less experienced climbers have a common flaw that disqualifies them. *They haven't thought about or prepared themselves for the demands of the mountain they are about to ascend.*

They haven't considered the high altitude symptoms, weeks or months of acclimatization and myriad reasons why they might die and not return.

Many of them have never trekked at high altitudes much less on a peak requiring hours in what is commonly called *The Death Zone.* Instead they are enamored by the adventure, the acclaim and perhaps romance of a trek in the Himalayas.

Even those who are qualified, physically and mentally ready for such a task, understand and respect the weightiness of the demands of hiking in these dangerous ranges. Corners can't be cut. The perils must be evaluated. Every possible problem, concern and implication needs to be reviewed if there is going to be a successful result.

The same is true with personal mountains. We can't skimp, look the other way or pretend that our mountain is less demanding than it really is. It too will have its dangers, pitfalls and scary encounters.

Good preparation, knowledge and awareness lead to greater freedom and confidence later. Our preparation must include an accurate assessment of what we're facing.

## Define Your Mountain . . . In All of Its Ugly Glory

Remember: mountains are both beautiful and relentlessly dangerous. We must accept the reality of these extremes. High peaks can be magnificently beautiful but their splendor is usually accompanied by monumental risks and significant danger.

A focus on either end of the spectrum, however, is foolish at best.

Just raving about the gorgeous scenery is naïve. But only thinking about the negatives and possibilities of dying will lead to unreasonable fear and quitting the climb before it starts. Both tacks are debilitating and unhealthy forms of *denial.*

When we look at our personal mountains a balanced perspective is vital. It will be essential that we *truthfully* assess the mountain ahead, agree on both the positives and negatives, then move on and get going.

Keep in mind, however, that mountains typically affect us more on the negative side than the positive. As mentioned earlier, many mountains are not our fault, come along suddenly and can leave our heads spinning. We'll need to take some time to overcome the shock of our bad news and the new challenges ahead. Defining our mountain is something we will do best *after* the unnerving jolt of first hearing about it.

We must wait until we're not so racked by hurt, loss, disappointment and fear. Then at some point when we can think more clearly we will more adequately face the facts of our dilemma.

Bringing a spouse or good friend into the process is important and helpful here since someone else can provide perspective that is likely less emotional. Let them help you write a summary of what you're facing and answer some of the following questions.

## How big is it?

Nobody with any brains at all climbs in the Himalayas without knowing that the demands there are far riskier than any others in the world. Climbing above twenty thousand feet is a whole new ball game, one containing multiple glaciers, the potential for severe frostbite, moving crevasses and possible brain or lung trauma due to altitude.

To venture into extreme altitude without the proper planning, equipment and understanding of the physical demands is simply foolhardy.

In the same way, we must accurately judge the *size* of our personal mountain. Jackie's cancer was a big deal because of the elevated staging of her tumor and the fact that the cancer had moved beyond the outer wall. It wasn't a reason to panic but was a shot over our emotional and intellectual bow that kept us from a casual, let's-not-worry-too-much-about-it approach.

What's the size of your job loss, the relationship that has been trashed, the addiction just revealed or the incident causing so much fear in you or your loved one? Proper analysis will lead to the wisest next steps that I'll talk about in later chapters.

This is where key conversations are needed with at least one other person in the room so everyone's hearing the same story. Doctors, counselors, pastors and other trusted individuals can be helpful in making sure that we're understanding all that needs to be known about our struggle.

## WHAT ARE THE POTENTIAL IMPLICATIONS?

When we first learned that Jackie had cancer, our immediate question was, "*Is she going to die?*" And while it was gut-wrenchingly hard to think about, it was essential that we ponder that terrifying possibility. There are several reasons why at some point we must boldly face the unknowns, the overwhelming parts and possibly hard-to-hear implications of our climb.

For one thing, *we will prepare better*. We'll have considered most of the big, scary and hairy results and plan more carefully than if we just winged it.

I remember the first time I did serious whitewater rafting. The guide had to teach us how to engage high class 3 and class 4 rapids since we were going to also be paddling. We would definitely be active participants.

So, he instructed our group to actually sit in the raft *on land* while we listened to his commands and then responded properly. We rehearsed this over and over, again and again both on land and after we entered the fairly calm waters of the Arkansas River.

*It was in the still water that we prepared for the rough waters.* In the same way, we must prepare beforehand for the rough parts of our personal mountains.

But second, *we will be more adept at deciding where to start.* We must of course begin with the easy, basic part of the trail, focusing on what comes first, not the whole mountain (I'll cover much more in chapter eight about conquering the trail in smaller parts.)

Prioritizing is where the experts in our world, the professionals, medical team, counselors, pastors, advisors, legal counsel, wise friends and others can be very helpful. Ask them to help you think through and manage your early steps, ordering them as wisely and accurately as possible.

Later in Jackie's cancer treatment she had a major surgery which would determine whether she would have a bag attached to her side for just a while or her entire life. Thankfully, the answer was the temporary version.

But to have spent time thinking and worrying about that before the other pieces of the puzzle were in place would have been a severe distraction and scare that we didn't need. We knew this more serious procedure would be coming but could put it on our mental back burner until closer to the time it was needed. Good preparation helped us make that decision.

## What Really Caused Your Mountain?

Last week John lost his high paying job of twenty-seven years. There's no chance he'll be hired back, his age now a major negative in his line of work. He could argue he was treated unfairly and his firing illegal, but the financial and emotional costs of that fight don't seem worth it.

John and his wife Jan not only face the discouragement of feeling like a failure, but also must now figure out how to cover expenses until he hopefully snags another job.

This is their new mountain. They need to look truthfully at their situation to fully grasp their need. It's a large peak since John was the major breadwinner. Thankfully there are open jobs in his field but his skills may be dated and worn in today's high tech-driven workplace.

John and Jan must now consider the implications of their predicament: Should they downsize, change their lifestyle in other ways, use their savings, sell major possessions, have John go back to school or pray for something to emerge quickly?

However, sometimes there are deeper reasons for our problems.

What I didn't mention in my story is that John lost his job because he had become hard to work with. Recently the usually kind, helpful worker had become a more annoying, *I'm-in-control* leader. Those who worked with him were showing dissatisfaction and resentment, not respect. They complained to supervisors who tried to talk to John and help him change. Sadly, that didn't work and he was let go.

You see, to avoid these hidden attitude problems and how they impacted the rise of his *Matterhorn* would have missed the more serious tumor within him. That cancerous growth requires significant attention as well if John is to really change.

John's loss of job was of course an issue, but *how and why he lost it was a far bigger concern.* To merely help John find another place to work would only serve as a temporary solution, not a summit-level one.

We too must take an in-depth look at anything that might have caused our mountain, especially the root that needs addressing in us. Counseling and coaching would help peek below the surface and find the real culprit.

Your mountain may include an addiction. However, just quitting drugs, drinking or your runaway spending isn't the whole answer. Real change will involve learning to see yourself differently, more positively, so that you don't need the painkilling that your addiction afforded you.

Sometimes some serious emotional surgery is needed if a mountain is going to be overcome.

## What Are The Dangers?

I distinctly remember the months before Tim and I climbed *Long's Peak*. We studied the routes, read numerous guides and manuals about it and talked to people who'd climbed it. If only *You Tube* had been around then we would have watched every video we could find!

We needed to know the messy truth about what could happen if we weren't careful. Remember, *Long's Peak* is considered the deadliest (though not the hardest) of all the 14ers in Colorado. On *Long's Peak* we needed to think beyond the *Keyhole*, the first big marker and turning point that starts the actual climb up the backside of the mountain. It was also my stopping point as an eleven-year-old.

Another threat was running out of water and if we did empty our supply where would we find more? The answer by the way is *nowhere*. You have to bring your own. *Was there any risk that would stop us from going on? What if one of us got hurt? What if we were unprepared and didn't know what to do next?*

Knowing the big picture and determining what could go badly also helps prioritize what needs to be a concern right away and what can wait. Carrying all those worries with us will just weigh us down.

Which leads to one final piece of our mountain assessment, one often overlooked during our anxiety, fear and concern when a mountain shows up.

## Evaluate Your Resources and Assets

This is an easily ignored facet of climbing preparation, especially when people are first made aware of their mountain. They feel overwhelmed and can immediately think that conquering something of such magnitude is way beyond their abilities.

When Jackie's cancer was revealed and confirmed, we were overwhelmed thinking about all that would be involved and required. We had never climbed this trail before and the task seemed far beyond our experience and emotional capacities. And in reality, many big peaks in life are impossible to ascend at least by yourself.

It's important to realize that we do have resources, that there are other people available who can help us, give us wisdom, encourage us along the way and provide virtual *ropes and carabineers* to aid our climb.

First there are *informational resources* that can add to our knowledge and strategy, show us how to overcome and determine a pace that will be sustainable. There's something energizing when you realize you are not alone and that the resources for overcoming today are greater than they were even five years ago.

There are *people* who can also join your climbing team. I'll talk in more detail later about their role and who you might enlist. You may also have *time* on your side, more of it than another person who has a similar peak to climb. Your *finances* may be in better shape. Your *family* may live close.

All these options and more are potential resources. *Write them down.* Think about even the smallest of assets. The list may be longer than you think. I'll bring you back to this point later so just get your list started for now.

Yes, your mountain is probably quite real and surprisingly high. It may appear to be a *Matterhorn* or worse yet, a *K2* or *Mount Everest* in the Himalayas. In the upcoming chapters I'll talk about the specifics for making your way up and over a peak like yours. But for now, honestly look at what your mountain is made of. Stare it down.

That peak has no right to steal your joy, purpose or upcoming plans to make some sort of difference. To let the size of your mountain keep you from success would be like handing your future away on a silver platter.

Looking the other way, living in denial or pretending that your *Everest* is some walk in the park won't help you. You'll only be that much more overwhelmed and discouraged as you encounter the difficulties later. And you'll likely quit at some point.

But if you'll do your homework now, face the challenges of the climb, reconnoiter your assets and prepare well with the help of others and your faith, you'll soon be at the trailhead ready to get on your way and head for the top!

*Things To Think About In Chapter 2*

What are the aspects of your mountain that scare you the most?

What are some of the resources you've discovered that could help you up the trail?

What do you still not know about your mountain that you need to research with someone or somewhere so you will feel more at peace?

Who do you know who has been up a similar trail who might be a help to you now and later?

Are there *experts* who you still need to get advice from who will bring clarity to your task? I.e. medical, counseling, faith, financial, legal, etc.?

# CHAPTER 3: YOUR CLIMB AND STORY ARE UNIQUE (AND WHY THAT'S OKAY)

*Today you are You, that is truer than true. There is no one alive who is Youer than You.*
***Doctor Seuss***

Alan, a thirty-something businessman, lost his father in a car accident. There was no chance to say goodbye, enjoy one more special moment or make a final memory. One day dad was there, the next morning he was gone.

Along with his wife, Morgan, Alex and other family were immediately thrown into the angst-filled demands of planning a funeral, making emotional calls to those who hadn't heard and explaining to their children what happened in terms their young minds could understand.

Their mountain became a sheer, treacherous wall of grief: shock, denial, anger, and depression in no prescribed order or frequency. They understood that resolution and moving forward could come farther up the trail, but for now couldn't imagine what that would be like.

Their climb was going to be a prolonged, emotional, lengthy expedition through conflicting emotions, increasing difficulty, exhausting responses and a huge dose of the unpredictable. Most grief is littered with swirling waters, dark places, hundreds of unknowns and gut-wrenching emotions. Their mountain would be a tall one.

Like climbing, grief is also experienced uniquely. There are common principles that can manage it or hold it back but each person ultimately walks their own path to deal with loss. Like jet lag, you can soften it but you can't avoid it!

Psychologist Carl Jung wisely said,

*The shoe that fits one person pinches another; there is no recipe for living that fits all cases.*

The same is true for grieving, struggling and yes climbing. There are no collective recipes for overcoming every mountain.

There are principles, common threads, wise choices and suggestions that can be beneficial on most climbs. I'll highlight and explain several in this book. But even they can vary in their order, timeframe, intensity and usefulness.

That's why we must accept that our climb, even one similar to those I've illustrated, will stand on their own so we will be unwise to simply mirror someone else's journey.

In fact, as you find people to walk with you, those who have experienced part of or a significant portion of your journey, make sure they also understand individuality. They must embrace the wisdom, demeanor and patience required to let your climb follow its own trail.

People who think that they have *easy answers* aren't the kind of fellow-strugglers and climbers you need accompanying you! They may mean well but in the end their words and attitude can become just as toxic as your struggle.

Be aware and alert for comments comparable to these that come from a potential helper,

*"You know, my doctor (or therapist or lawyer or pastor or . . .) said that I should _______________________. When I tried that everything improved."*

This type of sentiment is a vivid warning signal telling you to remove that person from your list of helpers and run the other way! *Rubber stamp caregivers* as I call them won't inspire you to understand your situation and respond to the nuances of your journey.

Instead they'll likely irritate and annoy you as they push for their tightly held *prescribed and proven* methods that they believe must become yours.

They may even add guilt to the mix by suggesting their plan is also God's plan. Who can argue with God, right? Or they'll suggest that their overcoming play worked for them so it will for you. In their minds, the answers are black and white minus any gray. They don't comprehend the layers of complicity that make everyone's journey an individual one.

I suggest you thank them for their concern and move on.

## STANDING APART FROM OTHERS

I've talked a lot about *The Matterhorn* a stupendous needle of rock that juts into the sky near the Swiss-Italian border city of Zermatt. There is really no other mountain quite like it in the world. Its jagged, horn-like shape makes it especially difficult because of its steep walls and dangerous rock that climbers face from the very start.

There are no twenty-mile hikes to Camp 1, gradual sets of switchbacks or fields of boulders to navigate before the really tough parts begin.

The operative word from the beginning is UP! Yes, Switzerland's most prestigious peak is beautiful but deadly though dwarfed in height and difficulty by the world's tallest and toughest peaks.

Not surprisingly, the techniques of higher altitude climbing generally don't work on *The Matterhorn*. Some of the best mountaineers on *Annapurna* or *K2* in the Himalayas may be at a disadvantage in Switzerland.

In the same way, our personal mountains will share common ground with others but incorporate major differences outnumbering the similarities.

I've recently taken up golf again and one thing I've noticed through my lessons and watching professionals is that golfers, though very talented, don't all hit the ball exactly the same way. There are fundamental basics that every good to great golfer *must* master, but each player can have his or her own style and be successful.

Phil Mickelson hits the ball very differently than a Fred Couples or Bubba Watson and yet they are all high level professionals. Phil's swing is smooth and fluid while senior golfer Couples follows a herky-jerky path from his shoulders to the ball. Bubba never took a lesson in perfecting his high-arching swing and incredible distance. But to exactly copy any of them might actually hurt an amateur!

Climbing works the same way. Everyone will have his or her own pace, pattern and form. No two climbers will tackle their citadel using the same exact route, speed, equipment or other resources. That's why we need to be okay with our unique perspectives concerning progress as we head up our trail.

Let me talk about how to make your distinct trail work for you. Remember, your journey will never look exactly like that of another climber. It will wind its own way up your mountain determined by you, the person leading the journey.

And you don't need to defend your choices. Some will argue that their way, journey and ultimate direction is best but no, your framework is what is best for you! Don't let anyone tell you otherwise.

Stay your course and plan. Here are some key areas to keep in mind as you do.

## Unique Aspects of Personal Mountains

*Your timeframe will vary.*

Wouldn't it be great if every time we faced a problem we could throw all the variables into a simple, predetermined formula and calculate a perfectly timed plan to solve it?

Maybe someone could invent an app that we could download to our phone for those situations. Unfortunately, life and its many challenges don't work that way. Mountain climbing certainly doesn't.

When Jackie and I bagged *Grey's Peak*, her pre-cancer mountain, we needed over nine hours to top out and return to our car.

The average experienced, stronger duo such as my son and I would have probably completed the trek in closer to five hours.

El Capitan, one of the hardest technical rock walls in the world takes most experienced climbers three to five days to ascend, often requiring sleeping overnight twice while suspended hundreds of feet in the air. (Be careful getting up in the night for a drink or to use the bathroom!)

However, Alex Honnold, solo free climber extraordinaire, conquered it with a partner in several hours, still a record as of this writing. He did a similar shorter version without ropes, all chronicled in the now well-known *Free Solo* documentary. Of course, his climbs might have been different had they encountered bad weather, strong winds and/or unforeseen personal physical challenges.

Many factors, some unpredicted, some planned will determine how long a personal summit climb takes. Grieving, healing, compromising, mediation, job seeking, overcoming addictions, etc. usually necessitate extra amounts of time and effort as well.

Consider two grieving women who each lost their spouse at an early age. Their response times can vary dramatically. After a year, Carol has started to date, put her deceased husband Alan's things in storage and is wrapping up her time in a support group.

She still hurts from her loss, but in twelve months or so has begun to take significant steps forward relationally and professionally.

Andrea, however, remains a mess after a couple of years. She can't get rid of any pictures, take his clothes out of the closet or remove more than a couple of his prized possessions from the house. It is still all too painful!

She tends to spend more time at home than venturing out to church, community events or family gatherings.

Unfortunately, as alluded to earlier, those with similar past experiences to ours may suggest that the timetable they followed to their summit is what we should use as well. These fellow strugglers usually have good intentions but their advice is rarely helpful or accurate and can lead to discouragement, even shame. As the person hearing their advice, we can begin to think, "*They got over their struggle in a year. Why can't I?*"

But they're not the same person as us. We'll tackle our mountains with significant differences in the process and that's okay.

Most of the main characters in the Bible faced major personal battles. Their journeys to heal, grow in faith, get ready for ministry, restore relationship and become who they eventually became were significantly different in length.

If you're a faith person, you know that God understands our unique personalities, lifestyles, circumstances and impact possibilities. In fact, He made us to be distinct and allows the timing of our summits to unfold in ways best suited to us not a formula.

Like these Bible heroes, it will often take a major mountain and the time to conquer a personal struggle to get us where we need to be. But because of the challenges faced now we can confront bigger things immediately and in the future.

We're wise to let life have its way and accept a journey length that fits who we are and the direction we want to go. Life offers no promises that the mountains we're asked to climb will be easy (or short) ones. Neither should we desire to settle in the valley and miss out on an accomplishment that could literally change our lives.

*Your strategies and methods won't be clones of others'*

In the same way people often place their timetable template over ours, suggesting that their methods – cancer treatments, marital strategies, job contacts, etc. - should be ours as well.

Of course, there may be wisdom in their advice. It's possible that you could find success using their insights. But it is more likely that your hike will still vary from theirs. The bottom-line? *Never get talked into totally copying another person's journey!*

Like my golf illustration, your approaches and strategies for success will differ too. They should be diverse because you're unique.

This concept becomes particularly poignant when people pray for your mountain to either go away or be overcome. The truth is that the same number of passionate, caring people may pray for two similar situations but the end result can be very different. Which leads to . . . .

*Your results may differ.*

Jessica was the beautiful eighteen-year-old daughter of good friends of ours. She loved Jesus and wasn't afraid to tell anyone about it.

She attended a Christian Bible college for one year and was looking forward to obtaining her degree in ministry. But one night from out of nowhere her head became wracked with pain. Running through the house screaming, Jessica soon fell unconscious and was rushed to a local hospital.

She was later transported by air to a more advanced trauma center where the medical staff did everything they could to save her as thousands prayed.

Jessica died a week later.

Kathy, a mother of three older children, was also rushed to a hospital, unaware that she was involuntarily and wildly moving her arms and legs. No one knew why.

Something was occurring in her brain but the cause became an ongoing mystery even to the medical team. Thousands also prayed for her while she slipped into a coma. But one day Kathy just woke up and was soon normal again.

Two scenarios. Thousands of prayers prayed for both. Very different outcomes. One led to celebration, the other to grief.

The misguided implication by some is that if we just pray like they prayed we'll receive a favorable answer to our petitions. Their argument is that sincere prayer alone got them a new job, restored relationship or financial blessing.

And yes, as a person of faith, I too believe that God can provide that way! You may or may not. But the journey and results aren't equal for everyone. Jessica and Kathy are just one example of the potential disparity in results.

Thankfully the God I know does choose to heal, bless and provide for many individuals or families and often does so quickly.

However, He also lets others experience deep valleys or walk up tall, steep, demanding pathways before there are results. And sometimes those outcomes aren't the ones they prayed for.

Recently the great evangelist and national pastor Billy Graham passed away at age ninety-nine. He was beloved by millions and personally played a role in the salvation of people all over the world.

But his ministry, as wonderful as it was, highlights a vital truth. Not everyone who prays for and points people to God has the success of a Billy Graham. The results won't all be the same. Billy's life was never intended to be our life. He may have been one-of–a-kind and we'll probably never see another quite like him.

There's a section in the New Testament that is known as the *faith chapter.* There you can read about scores of Bible characters who *by faith* saw miraculous things happen. Some teachers, however, have erroneously taught that if we'll only have more faith like these heroes we must see similar results.

The problem is that later in that same chapter verse thirty-five adds the words, "*But there were others.*" The rest of the chapter describes a separate set of heroes who never saw the culmination of their faith, at least not in this life. They were tortured, killed and otherwise horribly mistreated. But they had faith, too!

Verse thirty-eight then says:

> *"The world was not worthy of them. They wandered in deserts and mountains, and in caves and holes in the ground. They were all commended for their faith, yet none of them received what had been promised."*

You see, I don't think God is going to someday ask me,

> *"Gary, why weren't you more like . . . Billy Graham, Mother Teresa or another pastor, writer or leader?"*

But it's possible that He will ask,

> *"Gary, why weren't you more like Gary? Why weren't you more the way I made you, using the gifts I supplied and the strength I filled you with to climb the highest of summits?"*

You might be asked a similar question or two.

The issue is not whether our journey compares to that of someone else's. The question is whether we've been overcomers. And if so, did we embrace our methods and final results as the right ones for us?

*What you value isn't the same*

Values differ from organization to organization but they tell us much about *how* things are done there. *Southwest Airlines* values being low-cost, using humor and being very friendly. *Chick-Fil-A* prizes good service and giving each customer a wonderful experience in the company restaurants.

As we climb mountains, we'll begin to shape our own list of the things we rank highest. They're ways of accomplishing our goals that work best and provide us with the most progress. They may be different than others' lists but that doesn't matter.

For example, when we hike Jackie and I have learned to value:

*Trekking poles*
*A brown bag lunch*
*Good boots*
*Adequate water*
*Taking our time, but being consistent*

And yet others will have a contrasting list that may contain some of our essentials while substituting others. For example, rather than taking one's time and being consistent, some hikers try to go as fast as they can.

Others bring only water to drink while many prefer energy drinks and juice. There's a group who climb up and back in one day while others love to camp part way. Whatever the case, you'll benefit in your personal climbing to choose those things that mean the most to you, help you physically (trekking poles and good boots!) and bring you the most success.

Just because someone used long-term counseling that included hypnosis to overcome his or her struggles doesn't mean you should. Just because a friend spent tons of time on her journey partying with friends, doesn't mean you have to move from being a wallflower to the life of every gathering.

Embrace your own personhood emotionally. Some people will cry more; others will exhibit bursts of anger, while many will hold everything inside . . . for a while. Jackie is the one in our home who more easily cries, often in the middle of one of our discussions.

But that is a release and help to her. It's generally her way of responding to difficult situations and conversations. However, at her dad's funeral I was the one sobbing. She felt the depth of her sadness later but what we expected from each other didn't materialize. And that was okay.

Emotions can of course be used or misused. Underlying issues surrounding deep feelings are best addressed by competent counselors or helpers. But some ways of responding are merely us reacting. We cry rather than blow up. Others write their feelings down while different goup likes to talk to a real person.

When we feel the pressure to change just so we'll be like someone else or make them happy, we're not accepting our unique values and likely won't respond in a healthy manner.

Remember, as you identify and face your mountain, it's okay to walk at your own pace and bring your own gear with your personal plan and objectives etched confidently in your mind's eye.

It's okay to be unique, be yourself and use techniques and abilities that can actually give you success in getting up your mountain. Your mountain doesn't look like anyone else's and doesn't need to.

And you don't have to perform or respond like others who've already climbed your mountain. Just be you. *"Today you are you, that is truer than true."*

*Things To Think About In Chapter 3:*

What ways of responding during tough times that you've seen others use do you think you are tempted to copy?

What have you heard from others that makes you feel guilty or less than adequate as you attempt your difficult climb?

Have you recently tried to get someone to handle their problem *your way,* the way you did when you went through a similar problem? If so, what would you do differently now?

What are some of the *values* you bring to your challenges including any mountain you're currently facing?

# PART II: BARRIERS TO SUCCESSFUL CLIMBING

# CHAPTER 4: SOME *DON'TS* WORTH REMEMBERING

*"It takes guts and humility to admit mistakes. Admitting we're wrong is courage, not weakness."* ***Roy T. Bennett***

It was my first full day at a rock climbing gym in Central Illinois. *Upper Limits* is a retrofitted set of large silos, each section fashioned into faux rock faces complete with handholds, various routes and descriptive numbers rating each one's difficulty.

Any serious climber knows that a 5.7 route is easier than a 5.12, even though the number as a whole is smaller. It's the number after the decimal that expresses the actual rating so that a .12 route is harder than a .7 one.

That day the sixty-five foot walls inside, though precarious, didn't initially look that bad. How hard can it be to work your way up those little nubs and ring the bell at the top?

I found out.

We first were taught the essential safety commands climbers and their partners must speak back and forth to each other. Instructors showed us how to tie a figure eight knot and be correctly hooked to the rope. It was also vital to know that our belayer (and vice versa) had us securely in his or her hands.

Checks and re-checks must also take place before anyone leaves the ground at this gym. If any of these precautions are overlooked, there was a likely suspension for the day by one of the staff.

When it was my turn to climb a mere 5.8, I was eager and readied myself to go. My belaying friend and I rechecked our knots and connections and subsequently agreed everything was done correctly.

I headed up the wall. Feeling confident, I carefully placed my hands and feet on the appropriate holds, concurrently wondering why this route was numbered as high as it was. I made sure that my legs, containing the biggest muscles and bones, did a lot of the work allowing my arms more rest for upcoming challenges.

The problem was that after about fifteen feet of climbing I was running out of gas. I had begun too fast and had little energy left for the rest of the route which to me had become 5.12. Those big handholds now seemed like tiny stones.

The tips of my fingers began to ache and chafe as I strained to keep my place. I never made it to the top during that first ascent. Later I conquered some simpler routes and at least felt a little more competent but technical climbing was considerably harder than I imagined.

During the following weeks and months I was able to conquer some of the more difficult routes. It took extensive learning, practice and avoidance of poor techniques that don't work on the side of a cliff. I realized that I needed to listen to the experts who knew far more than I did and could help me improve.

I also had to change my thinking about what constitutes success while adding a large dose of humility to my bruised ego. I learned a variety of things NOT to do when suspended scores of feet in the air.

Comprehending some of my new insights could mean the difference between life and death.

There are similar principles and guidelines for personal mountain climbing that can help us avoid wasting effort on strategies that don't work. Let me talk about a few of them.

### DON'T CLIMB ALONE.

I was watching the most recent Winter Olympics and saw a speed skating strategy that I've never observed before in any similar competition. A large contingent of racers began their race at the same time rather than paired with another skater.

Once the gun sounded the skaters in this new version took off as one group. The general idea was that they would skate together for a significant part of the contest to conserve energy, strategically draft each other for a while and then jockey for the best position to win.

However, during one women's race, a lone skater immediately emerged from the pack and began to skate out in front. She was soon ten meters ahead, then twenty, eventually thirty meters in the lead while the others remained as a group.

At one point it appeared that this solo skater's strategy might be enough to win. Maybe she could be far enough ahead near the end that no one in the pack could catch her.

But just as the commentators had speculated, she eventually ran out of gas and all the remaining competitors caught her, passed by and headed to the finish line. She ended up last. Apparently skating alone for most of the race was not the answer.

Going it alone is rarely productive in climbing either. On a granite peak, whether hiking or actually doing a technical route, other people matter. We need fellow participants to share the load and in some cases to belay us for our safety. We need others to encourage us to *never quit climbing,* to not give up and to be careful. You see hiking by yourself can be disastrous.

Many of us now know the incredible story of *Aron Ralston.* In 2003, while making his way through the picturesque canyons of southwestern Utah, Aron's arm became lodged behind a huge boulder that suddenly moved as he scrambled within the narrow passageways.

Alone, knowing the likelihood that he would die before being found, Aron carefully used his knife and did the unthinkable. He cut off his arm, allowing him to walk away from his 127-hour ordeal.

He was able to hike to safety and a hospital where his wounds were cared for and his life ultimately saved before he would have bled to death. But think about the different outcome had he asked just one other person to join him on that adventure!

Whether we've succeeded in summiting or just making it to the next checkpoint, other people provide us someone with whom to enjoy our accomplishment, share the incredible views and talk about the journey so far.

These fellow travelers may include family, friends, other strugglers, neighbors, trained helpers, medical staff. It depends on the climb. But one of the worst things we can do is think we must reach the top on our own. As the business maxim suggests, "*It's lonely at the top*"! So true.

Don't climb alone.

## DON'T CLIMB UNPREPARED

Jackie and I love to hike every chance we get. We'll take a casual walk in a flat, wooded area or more rigorous jaunt up a steep trail in the Rockies. Hiking does something powerful for our souls. Jackie says she can literally see the tenseness drain out of my body as we move through the day on a trail somewhere.

It amazes us how many people we meet even on simple hikes who are totally unprepared for the challenge ahead of them. We see individuals hiking in flip-flops. We are usually descending so we're quite familiar with the challenges coming their way. That footwear isn't going to cut it farther ahead.

These ill-prepared adventurers will no doubt miss out on any sense of accomplishment plus never enjoy the views and memories that they could have encountered had they come properly equipped. The right shoes or boots alone would have made all the difference in the world.

The harder the mountain, the greater the preparation required. Alex Honnold, the solo free climber I mentioned earlier, has most of the free climbing records in the world. Some people think he's crazy for climbing even some of the time without any ropes or other protection.

But Alex doesn't usually on a whim scramble up some unknown route hoping for the best. He often climbs the route several times *with protection* before he ever solos. He first learns all the nuances and challenges along the way. In other words, he prepares. In his own words . . .

> *"To be clear I normally climb with a rope and partner. Free soloing makes up only a small percentage of my total climbing. But when I do solo, I manage the risk through careful preparation. I don't solo anything unless I'm sure I can do it."* (*Forbes.com*, April 24, 2015)

Himalayan climbers do similar extensive groundwork, some of it before they ever reach Nepal or Tibet. Then more study takes place on the mountain itself for weeks, even months at a time prior to their push to the summit.

Personal mountains require similar amounts of planning when possible. Preparation can take many forms but here are a few key places to start:

*Physical preparation.*

You need to get enough rest, eat right, cut your schedule back and take certain obligations out of your life that tend to sap both your physical and emotional energy. You can't climb a mountain running on empty. The mountain will steal much of your fuel during the climb as it is so you must have a reserve.

Of course, any physical decisions, especially during a medical crisis, must have the guidance and wisdom of your medical team so be sure to get their approval and direction first on additions, subtractions or other changes to your physical regimen.

*Mental preparation.*

When mountains show up in life, our brains often go into overload. We soon begin to obsess over all the possibilities, dangers and other things to overcome. Sometimes people literally have nervous breakdowns or experience severe bouts of depression because they can't mentally and emotionally handle the demands of life in the thin *mountain air*.

I'll talk later about how to face your challenges and not become overwhelmed in the process. But the preparation phase can help if we'll do everything we can to filter out the unnecessary stuff that robs us of much needed reserves.

For example, we need to become better informed about how to effectively conquer our challenges. The experts and consultants in our lives can be a potent source for reading materials, potential supportive people, insightful seminars and financial assistance.

But we must make sure that even our information gathering is what I call *targeted information*. We can't go online and just start devouring everything we can find about our predicament. For one thing, it's not all helpful and more importantly it's not all correct! Mental preparation also includes providing ourselves with time, activities and people who can help us think about something else besides our mountain.

I remember Jackie and I often commenting that her cancer had eventually become all we ever discussed anymore.

And we knew that too much focus on our predicament wasn't going to be helpful.

When we could, we started watching funny movies or videos, listening to music we liked and just getting together with a few friends who would make us laugh and talk about something besides her illness.

Of course, the seriousness of the challenge will determine what anyone can endure, but it's important to look for ways to add fun and other special interactions to our lives even during the worst of the journey.

And let me remind you again about getting someone to help you look at what's beneath the surface of the mountain you're facing. That will be a long process, one you can do both concurrently with your climb and then add follow up later. But start now to do the wise thing and renew your mind. Real change starts on the inside!

## Don't Make The Climb All About You

Climbers have always dreamed of lofty goals. In fact, most of us who climb are rarely satisfied with our accomplishments as great as they might be. Award winning statesman and world leader Nelson Mandela, though not a climber said it well,

> *"After climbing a great hill, one only finds there are many more hills to climb."*

Sir Edmund Hillary was determined to defeat *Mt. Everest.* Ed Viesturs believed he could summit the world's fourteen highest peaks without using supplemental oxygen and eventually did. Alex Honnold says,

> *"Anytime you finish a climb, there's always the next thing you can try."*

Healthy ambition, perseverance and goal setting can all be positives in reaching new heights and conquering both peaks of granite and personal mountains. But there is something about climbing life mountains and taking the focus off of us that is also empowering, inspiring and healing.

I'll never forget Ann, who helped Jackie during her cancer struggle. Ann would regularly volunteer to take her to the hospital for one of her major treatments.

There is no sweeter, kinder, gentler person in the world so you can imagine how comforting she was, especially on those trips into the medical center as Jackie anticipated her not-so-pleasant experience.

But there's one more thing you need to know about Ann. *She also had cancer.* Yes, she served Jackie in the middle of her own climb because she knew the importance of not climbing alone. She also had a special understanding about what the journey might be like. Ann could connect with Jackie in ways most could not.

At the time Ann's cancer was considered terminal and that was now a decade and a half ago. Ann's still alive and doing amazingly well today. Her story has been repeated over and over by those who take what they have learned or are learning through their own climbs and pass those insights on to someone else.

Instead of merely overcoming their own obstacles, they concurrently invest in someone else and find new strength, blessing and fulfillment that they would have missed otherwise. In other words, *their summit bid isn't only about them.* It's shared, enjoyed and expanded through giving back along the way.

Perhaps you're not in the worst part of your struggles yet but you anticipate harder times ahead. You can remove some of the fear, pain and hardship by thinking about how you might serve someone else during your journey.

Are there support groups that you might join or places to volunteer related to your conflicts? Is there a church ministry that you could help with or individuals that you might be an *Ann* to? They're out there if you'll look for them.

Interestingly during the creation story in Genesis, God says, "*It is not good for man to be alone*". Or in Ecclesiastes in the Old Testament we're told that it's a tragedy of sorts when someone falls and there is no one there to pick him or her up. You see relationship, not just presence, is an essential component of the foundation and emotional support needed for any personal climbing experience.

This involves going beyond the fact that you have a fellow traveler with you. Yes, their company is important. But moving past the mere presence of another individual or two on your journey toward building relationship with them, supporting one another's successes and serving each other's needs can make successful summiting more likely.

## DON'T CLIMB BEYOND YOUR ABILITIES

In the *Introduction*, I talked about my failed climb of *Long's Peak* when I was eleven. While I so wanted to summit that day, my body had other thoughts. It had several built in limits as to how much altitude it could handle so when I reached a certain elevation it shut down.

I have a good friend, however, who has climbed *Long's Peak* at least seven times. (I'm not interested in another shot, but good for him, right?) However, I would guess that he never, if ever, faced the difficulties with altitude that overcame me.

I have another friend (I really don't have that many) who gets sick merely walking around Aspen at 7000 feet or so above sea level. Her limits are very different in the other direction.

We need to be cognizant of our personal parameters, fears, experiences, strengths and weaknesses as we head into a climb. When we unashamedly admit them, we can better accept that those restrictions could impact our success if we don't manage them well.

What are some limits that might slow us down or cause major problems as we try to overcome our personal *Everest*?

Here are some to consider as you get serious about actually doing your climb:

*Few family members living nearby*
*Limited or strained finances*
*Past bad experiences*
*Physical limitations*
*Unusual demands*
*Lack of education*
*Limited community support*
*Other recent challenges*
*Cultural differences*
*Genetics*
*Unsupportive family*
*Limited resources/experts*
*Needs for counsel*
*Other*

Wise climbers don't ignore their maximums. They embrace, accept and own them. They use them to their advantage and remain mindful of each one as they plan their strategy and route up their mountain.

I used to love to climb in the silo gym I spoke of earlier or other similar venues. The time was always therapeutic and while I left physically drained I was mentally and emotionally charged as well. The workouts helped refill me with renewed excitement about life and its challenges.

But a few years ago, I had to stop because the extra pain that climbing caused in my aging body became a curse rather than a blessing. Following a climbing session, I would spend the next couple of weeks aching all over.

The perks I once gained from climbing were now overshadowed by the intense pain in every muscle of my body. My limits were speaking to me and I needed to listen and respond accordingly.

We must do the same in our life struggles. It's okay *not* to be someone else, to not have their strength or resolve or ability to cope in ways we wish we could. Our humanity adds restrictions to everything we do but can also guard us on our journey and make sure we go directions we can handle.

If we're truly honest and admit we aren't everything we'd like to be, it could save our life because we won't try something we're simply incapable of doing.

Would I love to climb with professionals like Alex Honnold or Ed Viesturs? You bet. But my weaknesses would govern the kind of climbing we could do. To try and perform at their levels could kill me. Even so, at times we'll be tempted to venture beyond our abilities because we saw someone else do it or we long to be like them.

Don't go there. It's okay to not have the same capacities for climbing as another has. Don't get stuck because you can't keep up with someone else's standard. Keep going in spite of them. Remember *the view from the top is worth it*, no matter how long it takes to get there.

*Things To Think About In Chapter 4*

What are my most obvious limits that I need to admit as I climb?

What came to mind as I think about my preparation or lack of it for my summit bid? What could I do to better prepare now?

Who do I need to consider inviting to join me, to be an active, meaningful part of my trek?

What other resources do I actually have at my disposal that could help my climb?

# CHAPTER 5: NO MORE EXCUSES

*"Ninety-nine percent of failures come from people who have the habit of making excuses. "*
***George Washington Carver***

I vividly remember the night before our *Long's Peak* climb. Tim slept like a baby but I tossed and turned. For weeks I'd read scores of reports, summaries and descriptions about every route on the mountain, even those that involved technical climbing. Of course, I knew that we were going to be using the popular *Keyhole/Fried Egg Trail* but I wanted to absorb the big picture.

I scoured articles about *Boulder Field, The Trough, The Narrows, The Ledges and the Home Stretch,* all key sections of this challenging though easiest route to the top. I visualized us taking on each portion armed with a forty-year hope that my failure as a young boy could be redeemed.

I was going to beat *Long's Peak* this time having shown up as prepared as possible. I was totally confident that Tim and I would soon stand on the summit.

Since Colorado expeditions always require an early start we headed for bed before nine. As I laid my head on my pillow, darkness became the backdrop for a non-stop, relentless video reel that ran in my brain most of the night. The highlights contained what I worried about as I pondered the next day's challenges.

The panic that began to surge through my soul started an expanding list of excuses about why we should postpone my dream adventure for at least one more day.

For the next several hours I mulled over dozens of *what if* questions including::

*What if we don't have enough supplies?*
*What if a storm comes up that we couldn't anticipate?*
*What if we aren't strong enough to make it?*
*What about those ledges I've read about? Are they narrower than I thought?*
*What if Tim falls and doesn't come back?*

Myriad other questions haunted me as well (I only slept 2-3 hours) spawning more reasons why we shouldn't go.

*I haven't had enough sleep.*
*We can do this another time.*
*Maybe we need a guide.*
*Perhaps we should wait another day.*
*The weather could be dicey.*
*We're taking on more than we can handle.*

Those fears and accompanying justifications came close to not only shutting down our summit attempt, but any ascents on *Long's* the rest of our trip. Saying *no* then could have been the ultimate and likely end of my hope ever becoming reality.

But I was learning another important lesson that later helped me up other mountains. *Mountain climbing should always have a measure of fear at its core.* Healthy fear has no right to keep anyone from the top or to completely paralyze them.

Notice I said *healthy fear*. Healthy fear is a pondered and considered concern that things could go wrong. It's a cautious regard for possible uncontrollable events that are bigger than our abilities. People who climb with no fear often die!

Healthy fear with the proper preparation, thought and information gathering can actually help and co-exist with our commitment to conquer the mountain we face. The right kind of fear assures that we remain alert, on mission, focused on what really matters and aware of potential dangers but minus debilitating panic.

On the other hand, *unhealthy fear* leads to nights like the one I experienced before our climb. This unwarranted fear is conceived in poor preparation, ignorance and past negative circumstances that for wrong reasons shake our confidence and view of ourselves. It breeds illegitimate excuses that keep us from overcoming, winning, succeeding or conquering the trials that life throws at us.

Thankfully, the next morning Tim and I still headed for the trailhead, took on *Long's Peak* and as you now know, made it to the top. So let me talk about some of the fears and resulting excuses that can taunt us as we face life's big mountains:

## COMMON FEAR-DRIVEN EXCUSES

*My problem can't be solved right now.*

I do a presentation and have another book called, *What On Earth Are You Waiting For?** It describes how so many of us live life as though something in the future must happen before we can move on.

In reality, we become prisoner to future events and outcomes rather than free to keep going anyway. When caught in this trap we regularly dwell on thoughts such as: "I'll change or work on my mountain after . . .

*My kids get through school.*
*I get a new job.*
*I get married or have children.*
*We make more money.*
*My illness is gone.*
*The house sells.*
*I finish my degree.*
*We get our parents settled in a home.*

Get the idea? Any moving forward or change is rooted in *someday.* The problem is that someday rarely comes. And even if it does, there will be five more somedays waiting in the wings. We'll have to then delay moving forward again so those new somedays can be fulfilled or completed.

But all that time the mountain is waiting. You're tired of living in the valley and ready for a change. In some cases conquering your peak is a life or death situation or at least one of great urgency that can't be postponed much longer.

Your mountain needs attention *now* so you must start your attempt soon. Of course, you should prepare well and follow the other suggestions in this book but head *now* for the trailhead and get started. There may never be a better time.

*I'm not strong enough.*

It's easy to look at the size of your personal challenge or struggle and think that you don't have the energy, core strength or power to overcome it. So, let's start with a basic, but essential truth: "*You don't have the power to summit on your own!*"

Very few do. Remember climbing is a group effort, before the climb, during and after. There is a misguided phrase floating around faith and even public circles that suggests, "*God won't give you anything bigger than you can handle.*"

Sounds like a nice meme for a *Facebook* meme or *Instagram* page, but it doesn't describe the way things really work. The phrase should more accurately read, "*God won't give you anything bigger than He and others alongside you can't handle!*"

Not being strong enough isn't the issue. The better questions are, "*What other resources do we have available that will help us succeed? Who will be alongside us to help overcome the altitude of our mountain?*" Do we believe that there are people along the way who we can also call on as needed, ones we may not even know at the moment?

On *Long's Peak*, Tim and I were making our way up *The Trough* on the back side after the *Keyhole*. We had brought what we thought was enough water and Gatorade for the all-day hike, but we were running short. We soon met a team of young guys coming down who asked how we were doing and whether we had enough to drink. He could tell from my tentative response that we were clearly short on liquids.

He immediately took my water bottle and filled it with some of his. I'll never forget his kind act. Even if we're not strong enough (and most of us aren't) there are others out there who will help us along the way.

If we use the excuse that we're not tough enough to do this climb, we'll never start. We'll miss some very special moments when people like Ann or the young man on our hike pick up the slack for us.

There are people out there who are just waiting for an opportunity to help and we should plan to ask them. We steal a blessing from them when we don't climb or quit because we're uncomfortable with accepting assistance.

If you are a faith person, you know that the Bible says *God's strength is perfected in our weakness.* Without climbing we'll never give God or life a chance to show and develop greatness in us. Sometimes I think God utilizes other people as His pipeline for that greatness and progress.

By not climbing we never get an opportunity to test the *power of the rope.* The first time I ever did any serious rappelling, I stood at the top of an eighty-foot cliff in a climbing harness connected to two different ropes for the descent.

I'm not particularly afraid of heights but I definitely experienced fear of the unknown. *What if the rope breaks? What if I don't stop in time? What if I panic part way down and simply fall to my death?*

All those thoughts darted around my mind while I was still securely standing at the top of the huge cliff. You see I hadn't tested the power of the rope. And there was only one way to do that. My courage would have to break through my fear and join forces with the reassurance that the rope would hold me.

And the same is true for life's mountains. As I suggested earlier we must commit to trust Someone or Something bigger than we are. In my mind that includes God Himself. He is the only rope that will not break. We don't have to be strong enough. We must just rely on faith, people and things beyond us as we take that first leap, lean back and enjoy the scary ride.

In fact, the more we climb, the stronger we get. The more a swimmer swims, the faster they go. The more weight a lifter lifts, the more muscle they add. Getting stronger on a mountain is a *result* of climbing it more than a *prerequisite* to doing it.

*It will take too long.*

Let me clarify. I'm not a professional mountaineer or expert. Yes, I've summited nine big Colorado mountains, but I'm not even close to having the skills and experience of the elite climbers who overcome cliffs thousands of feet high.

I only know a little about belaying, climbing knots and the various kinds of gear that a climber will have in their rack of protection. I've never trekked in the Himalayas or summited anything higher than fourteen thousand feet. If you want expertise about technical climbing and even serious hiking consult with a pro.

But I do know this. Most climbs of any consequence *take a long time to complete.* Yes, there are the Alex Honnolds who put up speed records but there aren't many in his class. *El Capitan* usually takes days to complete, *Everest* requires months and the other major climbs are somewhere in between. Even *Long's Peak* can involve multiple days if you're climbing one of the harder routes.

Whatever the magnitude of your mountain plan on a lengthy journey. But never let that be an excuse to quit. All good things take a while. As the saying goes mountain climbing is much closer to a marathon than a sprint.

Think of a *superstar* that you highly respect – educator, athlete, business expert, musician, actor, politician. Did any of them just show up at their level of expertise? Probably not. There were decades of details in their developmental story that you have never heard.

When I was a teacher, I had several students who went on to athletic, educational and social greatness. At least one won a medal in the Olympics. Another played professional hockey. All I know is that they sacrificed multiple years of training, resources, teen experiences and time to achieve those impressive goals.

You see there is a temptation to try to summit too quickly which leads to errors, dangers and possible death. Rushing a result, thinking that you've arrived when you have not, can lead to worse consequences than you started with initially.

There are two words that most climbers know about but would rather not hear. *False summit.*

When climbing a peak, your eyes will often deceive you into thinking you're nearing the top. You can see only sky above what appears to be the high point so you think you're almost there.

But you're not. In spite of a weary body screaming, *"Let's be done with this!"* the rest of the mountain is behind the false summit and you still have a long way to go.

When we expect our journey to be short, easy or better than others have experienced, we'll likely find ourselves facing more and more false summits. And every one of those can deplete our energy, perseverance and commitment to finish.

Alpinist John Ohrenschall says it well . . .,

*"Climbing would be a great, truly wonderful thing if it weren't for all that damn climbing."*

Summiting requires climbing, climbing and more climbing. It's a long trek. Don't miss out on a victory just because it takes a while.

*I'm afraid of failing.*

For many of us who climb failing is our biggest fear. We don't want to tell someone about our dream ascent only to flame out and not make it. How will we live with ourselves if others succeed but we don't?

We don't want to get our hopes up, begin to imagine life without the mountain anymore only to find it still hovering, looming and reminding us we'll never win. We imagine what a waste it will be to work so hard to overcome and fall short of the top.

But remember multiple failures typically preclude the successes of any achiever. How many times have Olympic athletes fallen, crashed and been injured prior to astounding victories? Every one of those misses was technically a failure but they still held great value and importance to the ultimate outcome.

*'Never let failure discourage you. Every time you get to the base of a mountain . . . .you're presented with a new opportunity to challenge yourself, to push your limits beyond what you thought possible, to learn from climbers on the trail ahead of you,*

*And to take in some amazing views.*
*Your performance on the mountain you climbed last week or last month or last year doesn't matter - because it's all about what you are doing right now."* (Alison Levine, *On The Edge: The Art of High Impact Leadership*)

Leadership expert John Maxwell wrote a book that coined one of my favorites of his titles: *Failing Forward.* We must learn to let failure push us ahead, not paralyze; energize, not deplete; and teach, not tear down. Naturally, we'll mess up as we climb our life mountains but we'll be better because of it.

We'll join the human race and the thousands who've nosedived before us. We learn, grow and climb higher each time we embrace a mistake. Making mistakes isn't failure. Letting our errors keep us from climbing is. The question isn't whether we'll make mistakes. The question is how many?

My failure as an eleven-year-old on Long's Peak hurt me deeply but helped me immeasurably. I never forgot that experience so it motivated me for decades. But I also learned something about the mountain and what it would take to climb it later helping me prepare to tackle it as an adult.

*"Big alpine routes aren't exactly safe... You need to have your feelers out, and you need to be willing to back off if things aren't quite right. At the same time, you have to push through your doubts and fears."* (Michael Kennedy)

*Other people are unwilling to go with me*

Let me tell you something right up front. I wish it weren't true but it happens all the time.

When it comes to change, significant change, life change, there are only a small percentage of people who will embrace that journey with you. You may get far more resistance than cooperation, negativity than positivity and beating the darkness than shining a light for you.

In other words, not everyone will believe you can conquer your mountain or have any interest in helping you make it. Why?

Some people have never overcome anything themselves so why should they believe you will? Others try to speak for God and tell you He's not going to give you your summit. Many others don't have the time to support your expedition.

Sure, they hope you succeed but don't count on them to help you make it. Unfortunately, some of the naysayers will be part of your family, a spouse, close friends, church members or leaders, a neighbor, an expert who has helped you in the past but now is retracting their support.

While you would love to have a host believing in you, walking alongside and encouraging you, the likelihood is there will only be a select few you can count on to stay with you. But the fact that many will not care much about your climb or enthusiastically begin the journey is no reason to quit or not start.

This may be the first time in your life when you finally quit basing your major life decisions and changes on whether others support you, agree with you or actually care about how you turn out.

*It's time for you to climb your mountain whether the people who matter most to you are involved or not.*

There's nothing wrong with asking for their help. There's everything wrong with *demanding* it. Desire it, even pray for it, but don't require it! Your ultimate decision to summit your mountain rests in one place, one mind, one attitude, one determination – YOURS! Anyone who joins with you is a wonderful side benefit.

The good news is that there are people who will eagerly join your team, even travel with you, but who they are may surprise you.

They will often be those who you don't know well but who've been through something similar. They may be individuals that come into your life for some special reason perhaps as part of their own healing and progress.

They could be people who've never taken on a challenge as big as yours but they're going to try it because you are. *Be thankful for them.*

Your success in getting to the top starts and ends with you. Don't be overly disappointed, angry or panicky because of those who aren't as excited about reaching the top of your *Everest* as you are. Focus on those who *will* support, encourage and challenge you throughout your expedition.

This means that you never let anyone's lack of involvement stop you from climbing higher. Entertaining lame excuses is a recipe for failure. But when you are willing to say a resounding "NO" to any silly, unnecessary, fear-laden alibis, you are ready to leave the trailhead and head for your summit.

It may take a while, but *the view from the top is worth it!* Commit now to use the questions and practical ideas at the end of this chapter to help increase your readiness and ability to succeed.

**(There is a second, longer version called NOW that is a more detailed look at moving forward from a biblical perspective in Luke chapter 9. It is also available on Amazon.com)*

*Things To Think About In Chapter 5*

What are the top 3 excuses that I tend to turn to when I become afraid of moving forward in any area of my life?

What is the number one excuse I'm using now to avoid tackling my personal life mountain?

What people have I been demanding change in before I can move forward?

What can I do to show that their decisions aren't affecting mine anymore?

What is the next thing I need to do to get moving again, head for the trailhead or start up the mountain?

# CHAPTER 6: REASONS YOU MIGHT QUIT

*"Age wrinkles the body; quitting wrinkles the soul."*
***Douglas MacArthur***

Andrea's cancer diagnosis hit her and Carson like a ton of bricks. The bad news from Dr. Allenson revealed at Andrea's regular check-up was a total surprise. He'd suggested that extra tests were wise and merely a precaution but the follow-up visit revealed the discouraging news. Surprisingly, once the shock waned, Andrea and Carson felt confident they were up to the challenge of fighting her cancer and winning.

But further tests, appointments, talks of surgeries and other procedures gradually ate away at their initial positive, healthy emotions and peaceful reflections. Sleep became erratic, their minds wandered and they experienced more weariness, irritability and discouragement.

When opportunities to have fun came along they just stayed home. Two months into their treatments, Andrea decided she wasn't enduring any more poking and prodding. Carson, though sad, agreed with her decision, though he wondered if there was some *natural* way to get rid of her disease.

Andrea did cursory research online but nothing seemed to be an answer that they could live with so for all practical purposes they did nothing.

A year later Andrea died.

Ryan finished his seminary training with great excitement, anticipation and passion. Three years of study had deepened his eagerness to lead a local church, see people grow in their faith, care for one another and serve in the community.

Securing his first pastorate a couple months before graduation only confirmed that he was headed to a place God had picked for him. But three years later, Ryan was not the golden boy the people of Cornerstone Church first thought he was. Criticisms became more frequent. He started hearing more talk in the hallways about his preaching and leadership.

The original affirmative responses to the church's growth, more casual approach and the creative, vibrant services now appeared to more than a few as too much change and a slippery slope toward liberalism.

In response, Ryan and his wife, Char, tried for another two years to make slow, positive adjustments, discuss their concerns with leadership and re-visit the vision that Ryan thought he and the Elders had crafted together.

But nothing resonated with both the critics and the church as a whole. Ryan finally chose to not only leave but to accept a position in the business world that his uncle offered him. He was devastated that his dream of ministry might come to a screeching halt.

Carl and Paula had been married for twenty-seven years. Their kids were grown and doing okay though all three families had changed jobs and houses a couple of times already.

Nonetheless, the two grandchildren were wonderful and the proud grandparents wondered how they ever lived without these little ones.

However, the engineering company Carl worked for downsized about the same time that the marketing firm Paula helped supervise was bought out by another company. Carl then lost his job. The merger was a profitable one for Paula's company but she forfeited her leadership role and much of her high-end salary.

Over the next year, their finances were cut in half while they drained much of their savings to keep up. Carl's self-esteem took a major hit. He settled for a temporary, minimum wage position and then began to dull some of his pain by spending money they didn't have. Paula had her reservations about the purchases but also felt a little better once they had or did something new.

That year they bought a car on credit, took a Cozumel vacation and loaded the kids and grandkids up with extra Christmas presents. A good friend graciously warned them about their growing extravagance and offered to help them find better jobs but neither would listen.

They told friends and each other that they might just as well enjoy life and figure out the debt problems later. They weren't saving anything anymore, but in their minds they were getting by.

For all practical purposes they quit being responsible. Within three years their house, cars and any extra money were gone. Soon they lived in a cheap apartment. Their kids no longer called or gave them an opportunity to enjoy their grandchildren.

Life had changed dramatically and would never be the same. *You see quitting isn't usually planned.*

Very few people start a job, college career, avocation, hobby or ministry planning to forfeit it. Our intentions are usually to be the best, work hard, have great success and fulfill goals that we'd set out to reach.

Most of us, even if we initiate a task with the best of intentions, will face tough circumstances along the way that rock our world. And those challenges can so impact who we think we are that we quit our climb. The hassle, difficulties and pain are no longer worth the goal. Our response is often to just turn around and head back down the trail for reasons that I'll cover later.

But it's important and can be beneficial before our climb to be aware of several common reasons we may abandon our quest early on and ultimately miss the joy and other benefits of reaching the top.

What are some positive and negative reasons we might pack it in rather than persevere? Wouldn't it be tragic to not top out when the summit is reachable and the rewards so worth it?

## Good Reasons To End Your Climb

*Natural Dangers.*

One of the most terrifying sounds you'll hear on a mountain is that of an avalanche. Seemingly out of nowhere the side of the mountain starts to slide towards lower ground. In some cases these huge snow slides are planned and activated by experts to avoid worse problems later.

But whatever the cause, snow, rock and ice traveling at incredible speeds with destructive power can mean death or at best serious injury for anyone caught in their path.

Many mountain ranges such as the *Colorado Rockies* are also known for their violent thunderstorms that can form in an instant, usually in the early afternoon. There are as many, if not more, deaths from lightning in the big mountains as there are from falls or other related accidents.

When our daughter Amy was in high school, we attempted *San Luis Peak*, a lonely 14er in southwest Colorado, a forty-five minute drive from Pagosa Springs which was our home for the week. As always, I studied the various routes and we decided on a fairly accessible and doable climb.

Unfortunately, we didn't have a four-wheel-drive vehicle so we had to park nearly a mile from the highest trailhead. Nonetheless, we found a parking area, hiked the extra distance and eventually discovered a sharp right turn that would take us to the summit.

Because we were climbing mid-week there were less hikers than normal on our trail. Usually you'll see or meet dozens of hikers heading out during the morning hours. However, we only observed one male adventurer who was well ahead of us because he drove his jeep to the easier starting point.

All morning long Amy and I enjoyed the quiet, yet steep trek up the rock-filled trail and its relentless switchbacks. Soon we emerged from the wooded areas and headed above tree line. Clouds in the distance were darkening but nothing looked dangerous or headed our way so we plodded on.

Quickly, however, the sky became more ominous and we wondered if we should turn around. There was no lightning at this point (a sure reason to retreat) but my caution meter zoomed higher as the dark clouds billowed. Thankfully in the next fifteen minutes the man who had been ahead of us appeared and walked our way as he descended.

As he approached, I asked him if he had summited and he responded affirmatively. We were elated to learn by his report that we were only fifteen to twenty minutes from the top.

Energized by his good news, I asked what he thought about the clouds and possible storm. He replied that it looked like the worst was headed away from us and he wouldn't sweat it.

We shared our thanks and a quick goodbye then continued a methodical, even more deliberate pace toward the summit. But within minutes we heard thunder so I looked at my daughter and said something like, "*I'm not sure if we should go on. I think we should pray.*" And I did.

Within thirty seconds of saying *Amen* to a very abbreviated prayer a lightning bolt arced over the summit! Maybe it was coincidental, but I immediately said to myself, "*OK, God, we got your message. We're out of here!*" And we headed down quickly.

We were totally exposed to very dangerous conditions for the next hour or more so getting down was a huge relief. We were soaked to the bone as we got in the car but safe. Thankfully we had made it back to the trailhead area and our way home. Storms and lightning are dangers in the mountains that require we immediately give up our climb!

Rarer, but certainly possible, are encounters with wild animals, other climbers who need our help and fires that make the wisest choice a retreat and surrender. By all means when you need to do so, turn around and go back.

It was so gut wrenching to not make the top but that decision could easily have been our last one. In the same way, we can face *natural* dangers or changes that we are wise to respond to as we attempt to conquer the summits life throws at us.

*Change of Direction.*

Sometimes we may need to quit, even temporarily, because of a significant alteration of events, purpose, goals or the problem itself. During the full-year portion of Jackie's cancer journey our daughter Amy got married and we experienced another significant family challenge.

Amy graciously asked if we thought the wedding should be postponed. As we considered her suggestion, wondering if Jackie would be physically up to all that a wedding entails, we decided that with the help of others the festivities could still go on. We all needed something positive!

It would mean slowing down her treatments, even temporarily quitting a couple of chemo segments so Jackie could enjoy Amy's special day with family and friends. But we all pulled it off and enjoyed a wonderful day.

Your life mountains may also require you take a break or at least postpone your venture because something positive or negative happened that fosters a wiser course of action.

For example, if you're attempting to scale a personal financial mountain but one of your family faces a major illness, surgery or other life event, you may need to slow down or leave your climb for a time.

A new drug is offered by your oncologist, your financial advisor suggests you re-direct your limited funds somewhere else, an adult child makes a positive decision that changes the seriousness of the struggle.

These and myriad other circumstances can lead you to stop, slow down or at least change the pace or direction of your climb. Sometimes quitting, stopping, postponing a climb, even one that holds great passion, is a wise choice for a while.

*Miraculous Event(s).*

There are also moments when an unforeseen, something beyond the usual moment, manifests itself. As a result getting to your summit becomes moot. The mountain vanished! You may or may not be able to see or explain it but somehow this turn of events goes beyond your understanding. For all intents and purposes, you can cancel the ascent.

And while this book is not intended to be a faith or theology book, let me address the idea of miracles briefly in our context.

As I alluded to earlier, people of faith or no faith can respond in a variety of ways to mountains and personal challenges. And two extremes tend to show up in life climbing, both of which are problematic and unbiblical.

One extreme is placing a problem, issue, struggle and climb totally on God. In some minds problems are His to fix, heal, solve and provide for and all that's needed is to have enough faith. Instead of allowing others to assist them, these individuals ask for prayer. Instead of seeking counsel, they argue that God's guidance is all they need.

Some people with medical challenges concurrently appeal to more *natural* means and methods, but they still believe that God is going to overcome their struggle for them. They pray, claim, demand, shout, serve, worship, fast, give, attend special services and do a host of other things more than they did in the past. They sincerely believe their *Mount Everest* will come tumbling down without any personal effort.

To be clear, let me state with great confidence and commitment that *I believe God still does miracles leading to results that have no human, logical explanation.* Yes, He continues to heal, provide and guide us through even the worst circumstances. Jackie and I have experienced most of His provisions in some form or know people who have.

The problem comes when people suggest that we can *demand* that God respond to life's hardships in the ways we choose, that He won't ask us to climb, face hard things, need to overcome and perhaps have a part in the solution ourselves.

Some groups and churches are convinced that God has promised everyone who trusts Him a success-free, illness-free, need-free life. But that's not what the Bible says.

Jesus didn't heal everyone though He could have. Paul had a thorn in the flesh. Stephen wasn't protected from an ultimate stoning. And of course, Jesus endured the cross.

The other extreme is when people purport that God wants us to do all the work and fix everything ourselves.

They affirm that the Father loves and cares for us, but believe He will let us climb our mountain on our own. Their thinking is that when they face a challenge, they should get as much wisdom as possible, consult the smartest people and keep going until they overcome or die.

But there's a little verse in the book of Nehemiah in the Old Testament that provides a clarifying theological nugget about how we should pray, act and trust God as we take on the big challenges of life.

It's found in *Nehemiah 4:9.* Nehemiah was attempting to rebuild the wall around Jerusalem, a vital part of a city's protection strategy in that day. And yet many of the local leaders were not happy about his efforts and at this point in the narrative are on their way to stop Nehemiah and his crew.

In fact, in chapter 4 Nehemiah becomes worried about what may happen next. That's the context for this helpful phrase in chapter four, verse nine.

*"So we prayed and we set up a guard."*

Yes, they prayed, they sought out their God for help, but also put soldiers in place to assist in fighting off the challengers.

The idea here seems to be that they did everything possible they could to protect themselves and yet also prayed for God to intervene. Apparently both actions were important and within God's ultimate plan.

As we climb our personal mountains, we should seek out the best doctors, equipment, financial advisors, counselors and guides to bring with us up our mountain while, if people of faith, trusting that God will either do a miracle or give us the wisdom, safety and guidance we need.

So, we've seen that there are reasons to quit and allow our trek to be laid aside for a time. There's no shame in that, especially when wisdom in doing so wins the day. While our feelings can be misleading, sometimes you've just got to trust you gut!

However, there are also illegitimate reasons that can stop us from victory, from overcoming because we turned back too soon. Let's look at several.

## Poor Reasons To Quit or Turn Around

*Because the climb is getting harder, not easier*

If you've ever climbed or hiked in elevations above five thousand feet, you've noticed your breathing becomes more labored the higher you go. I alluded to the decreasing oxygen levels earlier in the book.

Deeper investigation will tell you that air at zero feet above sea level contains about twenty-one percent oxygen, while at five thousand feet diminishes to eighteen percent. That's a fourteen percent decrease. At fourteen thousand feet the air thins to only twelve percent oxygen, just above half the amount at sea level.

Therefore, on a granite peak reaching a higher altitude actually puts more strain on the lungs, respiration and one's mental condition due to the reduced oxygen content. In other words, getting closer to the top doesn't make things easier.

In the same way, our personal mountains may require more from us as we get closer to our goal. Of course, personal problems don't necessarily present the drastic physical effects of rarified air. Nonetheless, getting nearer to our objective can wreak some havoc or add surprising stress to our trek.

For example, many times the people who have been helping us climb see their influence and involvement with us eroding as we improve. They can begin to respond curtly, even angrily because they can't help us or spend time with us as they once did. They may actually grieve our improvement, become more demanding or just abandon us completely. (See *chapter eleven* for more about this dynamic when back at sea level).

Sometimes our energy and strength will lag because we've been pushing hard for so long that we're out of gas and the perseverance to continue to the top.

Ironically, climbers on *Everest*, due to their lack of oxygen and the extreme altitude, can become delirious and lose their will to merely take one more step. Many have died with no more energy left while a fellow climber begs them to get up. We can face similar high-altitude experiences near the end of our personal climbs even though we've almost made it!

We must anticipate and prepare for these possibilities. It is wise to invite people who we trust and know care about us to prod, challenge and encourage when they see these hardships rear their heads toward the top. Don't be surprised that those last steps to the summit may be the hardest ones of all!

*Because we're willing to settle*

Who in America and much of the world today doesn't know that Michael Phelps is now the most decorated swimmer of all time? But imagine him making the final turn during one of his later gold medal swims thinking, "*You know, I already won a gold medal, in fact I've won quite a few. I'm already the best swimmer in history. I'm just going to take it easy, leisurely swim the last fifty meters and call it a day.*"

That would have never happened, right? No way. And how tragic for Michael, his fans and the swimming world in general if it had. Michael, though still great at the time, would have been settling for less than he could be.

Thankfully, he never chose that option but pushed himself to the end of every race even in his final Olympic Games. In several of his last swims he finished mere hundredths of a second ahead! He obviously went all out!

You see we have to decide ahead of time that we're not going to settle or be okay with just being okay. There have been times on mountains where I've been so tired that I had to count every ten steps, stop for five seconds, then do another ten steps, stop for five seconds and keep repeating the pattern until I made it.

It was torturous at times but I committed to reach the summit *before* being tempted to give up. Of course, this is another reason why it's extremely helpful to have someone climbing with you to push you onward when the air gets thin.

But no matter the situation, a bail out must never be an option merely because we think we don't have anything left to give.

Earlier I mentioned watching the recent Winter Olympics. While there were many incredible moments of courage, strength, determination and skill, there was one climax that stood out above the rest for me.

Kikkan Randall and Jesse Diggins were competing in the final women's cross–country skiing race, a two-person relay where they would alternate laps with each other until the end of the race.

And while these competitions can become quite boring especially early on, the sprint to the finish will go down in history. Randall completed her final lap admirably but the American team was still behind. Diggans then took over.

When she started the homestretch, she was barely in second place with one racer left to beat. She and that nearest competitor, Stina Nilsson of Sweden, traded the lead back and forth as they headed for home. Diggins moved ahead at first, then fell back by perhaps a foot but never more.

Both skiers gave everything they had for the last several hundred yards, at one point using extra strength from somewhere deep within to climb a steep hill just before the finish.

In the end Diggins crossed the finish line nineteen one hundredths of a second before Nilsson! It was so close that her teammate Randall, waiting at the finish, wasn't sure who won until she looked at a scoreboard above the grandstand. Then a number "1" showed next to the words, *United States.* They did it.

Diggins and Randall had won the first women's cross-country medal in U.S. history and the country's first cross-country medal for any gender in 42 years! Why? Because they didn't settle and didn't quit even when they thought they had nothing left.

Mountains, especially for those new to climbing, have a way of sapping your strength making you believe that you have nothing more to offer in your fight to conquer the weather, altitude and corresponding dangers.

But we almost always have reserves in the tank. We may be slower than the next person and might need the help of another but we can't turn around just because we think we're out of resources. In fact, if you happen to follow Christ, you can call on God who lives within you to connect His strength to yours.

As I touched on earlier, God said in the New Testament that His strength is perfected in our weakness. So give Him a chance to provide you with the extra power you may need to finish your mountain assault.

*Because someone you know quit.*

When a host of people turned around on Everest in 1996, they saved their lives. They listened to wise people who knew better and didn't succumb to the urgency, pride and false beliefs that took the lives of many others that fateful day. Remember there are times to turn around.

One of the brave rescuers on Everest was Ed Viesturs whose accomplishments on the world's highest peaks I highlighted in a previous chapter. He knows what he's talking about when he says,

> *"It's a round trip. Getting to the summit is optional, getting down is mandatory."*

However, sometimes climbers turn around for the wrong reasons. Fear and the unknown win out over reasoning, determination and good planning.

When we're struggling up a life mountain, it's important to have a significant number of people around us who will help us maintain a healthy perspective about how we're doing. But in the process we need wise friends and family who know us best and won't allow us to let the actions or inactions of others keep us from finishing.

When Tim and I were climbing *Long's Peak* we met a group of men coming down a steep section known as *The Trough,* a section I described in an earlier chapter. Curious about their success I asked them if they had summited to which they said a definitive "no" so I asked why.

Their leader responded that they had reached *The Ledges* section and didn't continue for fear of falling. They had families at home and didn't want to risk it. At that moment I found myself questioning whether we would go across even though I'd diligently studied that section and seen pictures.

Thankfully, a short time later, we met another group of younger climbers who assured us we could make it and that it wasn't overly dangerous even for less experienced people like us.

I am so thankful that we didn't stop because of one group of people who turned around. As I like to say, *the view from the top is worth it!*

We live in a culture where it seems like just getting by has become more the norm than it used to be. People want *instant results* rather than taking extended time to accomplish something great, important or lifesaving.

Nineteenth and twentieth century oil businessman and philanthropist John D. Rockefeller once said,

*"I do not think there is any other quality so essential to success of any kind as the quality of perseverance. It overcomes almost anything, even nature."*

Nothing could be truer when taking on our mountains.

Be ready for potential *walls* and discouragements you may face as you proceed. Yes storms, injuries and other things that could kill you are reasons for cutting your journey short. But don't let unwarranted events, actions or feelings keep you from overcoming your trial or challenge.

Walking up those last few steps to the summit is worth it and years from now you'll be glad you kept going!

## Things To Think About In Chapter 6

What kinds of circumstances, responses or hurdles tend to make you want to quit?

Which one do you think you struggle with the most? Why?

Write down a commitment statement now that describes your new response to wanting to turn around on your climb? How will you move forward after you face that challenge?

Spend some time praying for wisdom to determine whether upcoming circumstances are really *wise* reasons for stopping or not.

# Part III
# Getting To The Top!

# CHAPTER 7: SEVEN ESSENTIALS FOR YOUR BACKPACK

*"The wisdom of life consists in the elimination of non-essentials."*
***Lyn Yutang***

There's a prank most hikers and climbers have either pulled on others or experienced themselves. The joke is to gradually sneak small pebbles or rocks into the backpack of a fellow-climber as you walk behind them.

Of course, the trick must evolve slowly so that your victim doesn't notice you were the perpetrator and simply wonders why their pack seems heavier than before. If you work it right, they start to believe that the extra weight is the result of their becoming tired and yet continue on for a while without comment.

Ideally you let them in on the prank before literally ruining their day and then enjoy a good laugh (or argument?) together.

Carrying around unnecessary weights or rocks definitely adds more challenge to a high country expedition. That's why life climbing works better and more efficiently when we tackle our mountain as leanly as possible. We must not allow unnecessary extras into our physical, mental, spiritual and emotional *backpacks* that can weigh us down.

On the other hand there are items that we are wise to include. Over the years Jackie and I have developed a list of things we now bring along on every hike. We used to take other things with us, believing they would be useful but discovered we rarely used them. They stay home now.

And while there will be some variation from person to person and hike-to-hike I think the items below are worth bringing as you tackle your personal mountains.

You can add your own extras and preferences but don't omit these.

## *BACKPACK* ESSENTIALS FOR LIFE CLIMBING

*Several important phone numbers.*

Remember my earlier warning: *It's dangerous to climb alone!* We may not need someone with us every step of the way but we'll benefit big time from friends and acquaintances on speed dial who we can call at a moment's notice.

Why? Too stop us from turning around. Remember my earlier comments about how easy it can be to give up? They keep us climbing when we're so wanting to quit. Climbing partners even if they're not climbing right next to us can help us fight the war against our excuses.

Mountain climbing is often unforgiving, demanding and exhausting. You will want to give up often. In the last chapter we looked at some of the typical reasons why people end their climbs. However, a powerful antidote to quitting is having someone around who keeps urging you forward

In the process we must be sure that every person on our list grasps how vital their relentless encouragement and support are to our success. They have to understand that we might call on them day or night needing their loving, but firm reminders to keep going.

Ideally, they will be experienced life climbers but currently undergoing their own journey isn't a requirement. They don't have to have summited a peak as challenging as ours. In fact, effective companions can help us even if they've never faced a monumental struggle.

More importantly they must be a trusted friend, but not so close emotionally that they allow us inappropriate and ill-timed reasons to give up.

Their love must be tough and encouragement authentic. We have to be able to look them in the eye and say, *"I need you to be hard on me. Don't let me off the hook when I should be staying the course."*

Our tendency, however, will be to round up our besties, people who love us no matter what who don't want to hurt us by telling us what we don't want to hear. These aren't the people we need on our support team. They'll be overly empathetic, overlook our faults and give us a pass when we need a kick in the tail.

*A positive but realistic attitude*

In the 1996 *Everest* tragedy, sixteen people died when two professional guides allowed clients to continue to the top even though their teams were well beyond the agreed upon turnaround time. We can't know for sure what these experienced leaders were thinking but it appears they assumed their team would be the exception to the rule rather than victims of it.

Sadly, they were wrong. The result was one of the greatest mountain disasters of all time!

Yes, the guides were positive and optimistic, eager to make their customers happy, but they weren't realistic. We need to robustly pursue success but remember there are wise reasons to stop and turn around. Sometimes a mere gut-feeling can be enough to get us to wisely head down.

On the other side of the coin, many begin a climb and immediately think negatively. They're defeated before they start. Every aspect of the trail they don't like seems to deflate their energy, initiative and attitude.

In the next three chapters I'm going to describe triad of principles, an additional set of practical help concepts essential to tackling your personal mountain.

These lessons we also learned in the high country will help you stay positive even when the climb gets steeper and harder than you imagined. Nonetheless, it helps if you bring a large dose of positive thinking with you. That means anticipating success, imagining how great it will be at the top and considering how much better life will be if you progress or better yet get victory.

It's beyond the scope of this book to dig very deeply into why you might turn to negative thoughts more often than others. But let me mention a couple causes for you to think about.

If one or more resonate with you, consider getting some counseling, coaching or other professional input to discuss ways to break free of your unhealthy negativity. Also try reading a couple of the resources found in the *Appendix*.

## WHY MIGHT YOU HAVE A BAD ATTITUDE?

*One or more of your parents always took a negative view.* It didn't matter the issue, the bad always outweighed the good with them. They couldn't trust anyone and implied that you shouldn't either.

Rather than try new things, they tended to repeat the same ones over and over. Some moms and dads came out of homes laden with criticism so that's all they knew. Others grew up in difficult circumstances where no one was to be trusted so they don't trust anyone now either.

*You were often told growing up that you were less than successful.* Every accomplishment you gained they picked apart. If you got a 'B' they wanted an 'A.' When you got your Masters, they wondered when you would get a doctorate. If you bought new clothes they wondered why you didn't purchase something else.

*You experienced a number of significant failures.* You may have endured one major catastrophe, several significant disasters or a lot of tiny mishaps. It doesn't matter – your past has made you gun shy of pursuing big goals anymore. You'd rather not crash and burn one more time and disappoint yourself or more importantly others.

Whatever the cause, you have to work harder to be able to bring positivity to your journey. Of course, I'm not suggesting putting on a plastic smile and pretending everything's fine.

Instead, plan to look for the positives in your struggles, put the past behind you and begin to think in new ways about what success could look like now.

Another verse in the Bible says that transformation or change involves the renewing, the reshaping of our mind, our thinking. (Romans 12:1-2)

It's possible that you have been living much of your life believing that your accomplishments were what gave you value and worth. When people didn't recognize your achievements in a positive, affirming way you felt de-valued and insignificant.

It's likely that as you stand at the trailhead to your climb you could talk yourself into imagining another potential performance doomed to failure. However, a positive attitude, one that says, *"I am not bound by my past nor what others think, but rather by who I am today the person I was made to be,"* is essential in overcoming your mountain successfully.

*Extra clothes for layering.*

Anytime you hike above tree line, even in the summer months, you risk the possibility that the temperatures will fall sharply, accompanied by a stiff wind. I remember when Tim and I climbed *Mt. Elbert*, Colorado's highest peak, we ended up wearing every piece of clothing we had with us. At one point it was so frigid we used our socks as gloves!

We went from cool, crisp morning air to a freezing cold, stiff breeze in just a few thousand vertical feet and thirty minutes. That's why in the high mountains it's essential to include a variety of layers (i.e. long underwear, long-sleeved T-shirts, sweatshirts, fleece, etc.) to put on or take off as temperatures change.

Similarly, we need tiers of protection on our personal life climbs. We may not use them all but it's important to have access to the following:

*A spiritual layer.*

Think about finding a mentor, good friend, chaplain, other spiritual leader or mature person who prays for you, provides helpful Bible insights and practical application as needed. In fact having at least a couple of these mature, insightful friends would be best.

If you haven't particularly been a person of faith up to now, why not use this layer to dig deeper again into who God is and how Jesus wants to live in you and walk with you? You might learn that God not only made the mountains, but cares about you getting over them!

You can also find some of the best and most appropriate resources described in the *Appendix*.

Regarding spiritual helpers notice that I suggested a couple of helpers, at most two. Don't let your tribe become too big. Receiving too much input, even Biblical guidance, can become confusing, anxiety producing and discouraging. Pick people you both know and trust most about faith issues.

This layer requires competent individuals who are balanced, have a Nehemiah 4:9 (see the last chapter) perspective on prayer, trust God themselves and don't demand that life work their way all the time. They need to be *tough but tender*.

They must help you engage your faith without trying to play God! You might encourage them when they have sage advice for you to start their comments with something like, *"You know, I have some thoughts about that if you'd like to hear them."*

*An emotional layer.*

As I've suggested or implied a number of times, you are also wise to find yourself a counselor, therapist, people-helper or trained confidante. They should be a competent people helper who can offer emotional support, challenge your wrong or misguided thinking and suggest options for the many difficulties and feelings you might experience on your journey.

This person's guidance may overlap that of the spiritual layer group. That's okay. But people at this level are trained to dive deeper into places the spiritual layer team cannot and should not go. The book of Proverbs says,

> *"The purposes of a [person's] heart are deep waters, but a [person] of understanding draws them out." (20:5)*

Find yourself that level of skilled helper! There are many gifted and well-trained professionals and lay people out there.

Take the time to research some and even try out several. Ask around and get referrals and references. Your efforts will be worth it.

*An intellectual layer.*

Lots of people are smart, even loaded with information and detail, but far fewer are wise. Wise people aren't just filled with facts but can aptly apply knowledge to everyday life. You'll want some of those especially astute friends at your side. They can aid you in evaluating information, strategies and ideas so you will climb more effectively and not get sidetracked.

In fact, depending upon the seriousness, size and intensity of your mountain, it is always helpful to have a trusted friend who attends key appointments, meetings and events with you to listen and observe. They can bring a clearer mind and less emotional distraction so that you'll be sure to hear the facts accurately.

Later when there are recurring questions and your memory is foggy or clouded with angst, they can review the details with you. It will also help to bring along . . .

*A journal and a camera*

When you confront a mountain there are always amazing, unforgettable views, vistas and experiences that will stay with you for years to come. Some of these moments may not need to be written down or photographed (though both are valuable) since they are so deeply etched into our memory.

These powerful images, often little surprises along the trail that we couldn't have imagined beforehand, will be shared over and over.

However, there are often less dramatic, not as noteworthy happenings that we shouldn't lose or overlook. They will show up as tiny, special glimmers of truth, joy and inspiration that could be lost forever if not chronicled.

In fact, they may provide the most profound lessons, challenges and encouragements of your journey. How tragic it would be if they just vanished because of sensory overload.

You'll need tools to capture them along your way. On an actual climb, a camera is one of our best and easiest ways to document our ascent. Some of the world's greatest climbers take pictures and journal their climb putting their notes on their smartphone or in a small notebook. Their written and pictorial efforts often lead to a book or article down the road that the rest of us can enjoy.

Life climbing needs similar tools. When Jackie was sick and we were forced into scores of consults, doctor visits, radiology reports and surgery follow-ups, I would maintain copious logs and put them in the *notes* file on my phone.

I would track the date of the appointment and highlight the specifics of what was said, a practice that ended up being extremely helpful when our memories were foggy.

I also wrote down meaningful moments, actions of friends who went the extra mile for us, Bible verses from my private reading and other anecdotes. I discovered that God seems to speak loudly at times but only whispers what is needed in other moments. Whatever you use to document your journey, be sure it's in your *pack*.

*Communication options.*

Only in recent years have we been able at high altitudes to use cell phones to connect with loved ones at lower elevations. More advanced expeditions have had access to SAT phones and other expensive technology for some time but that's not available to the everyday person.

It's been exciting to call Jackie, the kids or a friend from the summit of a fourteen-thousand-foot peak! Actually, when I phone a mountain-loving friend it's usually to brag. *"Sorry that you're not where I am right now."* It's also comforting to know that in an emergency there is a good option available to get help.

No matter the time, place or technology available on our personal climbs we must have options to communicate well. We may need to call for assistance when there is a concern or emergency plus reach family or close friends who will want to know how we're doing.

Most importantly we must have convenient and expeditious contact with the experts who are helping us up our mountain.

One of the biggest challenges for those trapped at high altitudes including team leaders is their inability to link up with others who could rescue them.

Even with high-tech SAT phones, their connections will tend to degrade the higher they go.

Rob Hall, in a heartbreaking last phone call on *Everest* in 1996, was able to speak briefly to his pregnant wife back home. Sadly nothing could be done to save him. Whether all those years ago the technology could have provided a better outcome we don't know, but the results were disastrous.

As we prepare for or begin our climb we must make sure we're using everything possible to ensure reliable connection and communication with our key teammates and resources.

Here are a few ways to do that: *The Internet, phone, small group friends, a designated communication person, best contact information for the experts on your team, emergency numbers, social media.*

Find the options that work best for you.

*Motivational rewards.*

Jackie and I have a special and perhaps unique way of keeping ourselves inspired on a hike. I'll talk more about this later but the core of our incentive is chocolate. Before every climb, we purchase a number of our favorite candy bars and hold them in escrow somewhere in our packs.

Their purpose is to inspire us when we get to higher elevations to make it to our next waypoint or goal. Let's face it. We all need a push sometimes. And I'm not suggesting that we necessarily use lots of calories and carbs to provide it. In fact, our rewards don't always have to involve food or dessert. A promise of a little time in a hot tub or a professional massage does the trick too.

But we can all benefit if we have a reward, treat or prize that we enjoy part way up our mountain. In other words, *we need to celebrate our progress.*

Now let me caution you not to shatter your goal on the way up. For example, if you're climbing a financial mountain and have made some significant debt-reduction progress, don't go buy a brand new truck as a present!

If you're climbing a mountain of overweight, have lost thirty pounds but have seventy-five to go, don't go on a hot-fudge sundae binge for a week or quit your diet for the rest of the month.

Rewards are designed to provide a *small* incentive to keep you going. If you're on a cancer climb, you might talk with your oncologist about a short break in your treatments so that you can enjoy life more for a short time of reprieve.

When you're working hard on a relationship, you could pick a concert, weekend getaway or other fun activity for the two of you to do together as a breather from your hard work. Reward yourself for progress but keep it helpful.

Make sure your prize is something that you will enjoy. A hurtful or unwanted incentive rarely motivates!

*A memento for the summit.*

If you ever climb to the top of *Mt. Everest* or even see a picture of it, you'll notice scores of flags and other objects individuals or teams have left there. Some represent their country of origin while others are in honor or memory of a friend.

Actually, many of them disappear in the storms that smash the summit all year long. The point is that each climber literally puts a stake in the ground at the top that says, "*I made it!*"

While such symbolism on our life climbs isn't required, I highly recommend it. Mementos can include an object added to your home, painting hung on the wall, a before and after picture, deed or other financial statement, diploma, first year sober pin . . . well, you get the idea.

Mementos do several things that will be well worth your thinking about and investing in:

*Mementos give us opportunity to tell our story.*

Often people will ask us about our keepsake and why it's there. During Jackie's cancer treatments we celebrated Christmas. It was a tough holiday for sure and that year we even had to limit our decorations. Neither of us had the energy or a clear enough brain to set up the usual holiday décor.

But one of our favorite Christmas scenes is *The Nativity.* At the time we only had a very simple set but we cherished it and usually put it up first. However, that year we decided to do something else after the holiday season. We left the Nativity set up in our living room!

All year long people would come by the house, see the baby Jesus, wise men, shepherds and animals and ask us about it. It was an open door to tell our story during Jackie's treatments and even after the cancer became history.

*Mementos remind us of our accomplishments.!*

Our mountain wasn't easy we overcame countless obstacles. Mementos are a great memory prompt about the challenges we just endured. It's easy to forget just how hard the journey was. They are a way to keep looking back down the mountain and seeing progress. More on that later.

*Mementos help keep us humble.*

It reminds us that our accomplishment wasn't all our doing. If we're people of faith, mementos invite God again into our story as we remember His wisdom, guidance and faithfulness.

In the Old Testament it was customary for the Jewish people to set up twelve stones as a monument to what God had done for them on their journey. Our memento can be our dozen stones and provide a similar visual cue to not forget God's provision and the help of so many people.

In addition, there will be individuals and groups who walked the trail with us, nudging us to never quit, who we need to remember and bless.

*Mementos can motivate us to succeed again.*

Hopefully we'll never have to summit a mountain of the same magnitude but if we do, our object, painting, sign or whatever can inspire us to take on another one as we remember overcoming the one now in our past.

## ONE FINAL CHECK

As you prepare for or continue up your mountain, look over your climbing supplies again and pack carefully. Take out anything that you likely will never use. Use the ideas in this chapter as a guide but also talk with some fellow travelers who have climbed before you. They may give you an idea or two for other pack items that will be unique and helpful to you!

Now it's time to get to the crux of the process. *What are the three most important keys to climbing your personal mountain?*

Climb on.

## THINGS TO THINK ABOUT IN CHAPTER 7

Which of the suggested backpack items are you most likely to leave out of your climbing gear? Why?

Talk about which items you think might be most important to add and why?

What things do you need to go and get this week and add to your supplies?

What other things have you found to be helpful or wish you would have had during your climb so far?

# CHAPTER 8: KEY ONE: TAKE ONE STEP AT A TIME

*"One may walk over the highest mountain one step at a time."*
***John Wanamaker***

When Jackie first called me from the doctor's office and shared his troubling diagnosis, we immediately knew we were going to climb another mountain together. But it wouldn't be a fourteener in Colorado, the magnificent *Denali* in Alaska or the stunning *Matterhorn* in Switzerland.

It would be a huge peak named *Cancer,* one that seemed more like *Mt Everest.* As we talked, cried and prayed during the next several days, our minds became cluttered with a sheer wall of appointments, tests, procedures and unknowns explained to us by the oncologist and surgeon.

Moreover, we felt a punch in the gut wondering if Jackie would live or die. We were overwhelmed by the scary implications of stage three cancer, feeling helpless and powerless to conquer such a formidable foe. We knew the doctors hadn't caught the problem early on, that some specialist had missed seeing the tumor during a recent colonoscopy and the cancer had spread beyond the rectal wall.

The odds of all that happening are very small. When it came to playing percentages, we seemed to lose every time. Not long after the diagnosis, Jackie lost the roll of the dice again, collapsing in the parking lot in intense pain because of her lung being punctured while her port was inserted.

But that's what so often happens when life hits us hard. The news is bad and then we receive worse. We hear of a moral failure, disaster, tragedy, diagnosis, addiction or torn relationship and all we can see or think about is the towering citadel now in front of us.

As we began to grasp the sheer magnitude of Jackie's condition and the huge obstacles her cancer had handed us, any optimism we might have entertained was sucked from our souls. Our resources were already depleted and we'd hardly started.

Why? Because we had first focused on the summit.

## A New Perspective

In the last chapter I discussed our use of chocolate to get us up steep mountain trails. Several candy bars served us well as small (but delicious) rewards to coax us through the next part of the climb.

But they are far more than sweet incentives. Those sugary morsels are vital components in our purposing to remain focused on the *here and now*. They help our minds hone in on the next switchback, the upcoming pitch or boulders in our way. The top is always beckoning, but we must resist its siren call to keep looking its way!

You see the first and most important principle for beating your mountain is this: *You must only climb one part of your mountain at a time!!*

The process is step-by-step, corner–by-corner, boulder-by-boulder, section-by-section. In mountain terminology, you complete the next switchback before worrying about the ones that follow.

As you certainly know by now, Jackie and are avid hikers. We will eagerly walk a number of miles on flat land or in rarified air. We love the challenge and the views we enjoy when we set a goal and pursue it on foot.

Consequently, we should have known that going through any personal climb requires putting one foot after the other. As a result we should have quickly understood that the way to tackle this new, huge personal mountain is to conquer like we do the goals we seek out on dirt and rock.

Thankfully, we started to realize the incredible wisdom of this first principle which is also highlighted in the words of the Bible as it tells us to *walk* in the Spirit, in truth, the light, etc.

So it wasn't long before we began to give more and more of our attention to the next event, the upcoming issue seeking them more as a journey not an end. We knew the summit still loomed but it now had less influence and power than we'd given it early on. The next doctor visit, test, procedure, upcoming surgery, follow-up, days of recuperation each became our new center for a time.

Our fresh single-mindedness didn't take the mountain away but provided what we could handle. And for each succeeding event we would concentrate our research, prayers, preparation, discussions with others, questions for the doctors and thinking in general on *only* that part of our journey.

We began to rest more in the reality that while God could handle all our concerns at once, we couldn't. We felt a freedom that we sorely needed.

In fact, we felt like we were given an emancipating permission to live in the *here and now*. We of course had to periodically think about planning, preparation and the big picture but those issues didn't dominate anymore.

They would be addressed in more detail when the right time came and our emotional tanks were full enough to handle them.

In fact, committing to only the next responsibility helped us find more enjoyment in each segment of the trail rather than bemoan the fact that we were still so far from the top. We discovered that there were things to see, relish, learn from and soak in during our climb that would be a shame to miss by running past them. I'll talk about that more in the succeeding chapters.

## KEEPING YOUR EYES OFF THE SUMMIT

So, what will *here and now* living look like? And what should you do to avoid the temptation to turn your eyes again towards the top?

*Be clear on your next goal*

Sometimes we add extra pressure or anxiety to our climb because our next task isn't that well defined. With Jackie's cancer there were multiple events, appointments and procedures happening in close proximity. Dates blended together and the huge amount of information we received often clouded our minds and added confusion to our already messed up thinking.

One helpful strategy was to regularly ask the medical staff to re-clarify what the subsequent procedures would be and when they would take place. In addition, we asked dozens of questions to make sure we knew exactly what would happen, why and for how long. How could we prepare, pray and dig deeper if we didn't know what was coming next?

When climbing it's easy to make the next checkpoint too ambitious. Or perhaps the place you're going to stop is unclear because many of the rock formations look alike.

On personal climbs make those checkpoints very obvious. That way you will better determine what should happen when you get there and whether more progress is possible or needed.

Determine who needs to be talked to, what issues are most critical and when will it take place. Schedule when will you check on your progress. Who will be there? What needs to happen before then?

Clear goals and outcomes help determine if you've actually arrived or not. It's one thing to know you have a surgery upcoming and to get through that. But the steps and evaluation times for a lengthy period of tests, procedures or rehab visits can seem foggy if we don't ask more questions.

Some struggling spouses might suggest that they will meet again in a couple of months to *see how things are going.* However, that's a fairly nebulous target that's difficult to evaluate. A better goal would be, *"Let's plan to meet on June 1st and consult together with our counselor about both our progress and next steps."*

If any of your aims are too generic or vague, you may end up covering the same ground over and over wondering if there's been any movement forward. Rather than making your next financial objective such as, "We'll be *a little more careful with our spending,"* try to craft it more specifically like, *"We plan to have saved a thousand dollars by June 1st."*

Unclear goals and plans lead to unclear measures that can steal from your incentive to keep climbing.

*Accept your pace*

I've climbed numerous physical mountains and I'm pretty sure of one thing: *I've never reached the top first.* There always seems to be people coming down while I'm still headed up. Many left the parking lot at two in the morning with their headlamps beaming, watched the sunrise at 12,000 feet and stepped onto the top as I arrived at the trailhead.

People often hike way faster than me, running past as I grudgingly fight gravity's pull. I've never been first, but I've often been last or at least close to the final person on the mountain.

But I've learned something over the years. *I have to know and embrace my own speed and endurance.* I'm simply not like the others.

I once climbed with a good friend who loves to do things by the book. He consistently checked his watch estimating what time we would reach various waypoints. He loved to hike at a much faster clip than I do and would usually be waiting up the trail as I plodded to his location.

At times I wondered if I should start going faster and I felt a bit guilty for my slowness. But I couldn't go quicker. To increase my pace would ultimately deplete my physical reserves.

Instead my style was to walk farther each time than he would. I intentionally made each step a very deliberate one. Eventually our different methods produced a varied result and that was okay. We weren't getting to the top together and that didn't matter.

Mountain climbing is not an exact science nor must everyone complete a route on the same schedule. Going too fast can sap one's strength while going too slowly may cause even the best climber to lose momentum. The higher the altitude usually means the pace will need to slow anyway.

Speed concerns typically come from people sharing their stories and experiences as though their capabilities should be normative for everyone. "*I was pretty much over my addiction in a year,*" a friend suggests. As a result, we wonder why we haven't conquered ours. Another person talks about being past their grief but you're not even close to okay and feel ashamed that you still hurt so badly.

Don't go there. The time a climb requires is up to us and the many factors unique to our climb.

*Don't freak out over what's ahead.*

During the months prior to climbing *Long's* I read everything I could about the *Fried Egg Trail* that average climbers like me use to summit. However, my reading also upped my anxiety level about the difficulties inherent to an ascent like this one.

Consequently, the closer the time came for our hike, the more nervous I got. In fact, when we started out I found myself looking ahead to what those dangers might entail. Remember my lack of sleep story?

That's the tendency on any climb, granite or personal. Our fears tend to distract us, pulling our energy and attention away from the next fifty yards of trail. Worrying ahead of time will not make each segment any easier.

In fact, our anxiety or panic can cause later sections to seem harder if our early concerns drain us of emotional and physical reserves.

This is where you may need your climbing *partner* (spouse, friend, child, parent, etc.) to bring you back to the present when your mind races ahead.

You might ask them to re-center you, talk specifically about the immediate portion of the trip or just say something fun to keep things light. Find a compelling and enjoyable topic to discuss in the here and now. Pray for the present challenges and give thanks for little bits of progress.

Which leads to . . .

*Celebrate little successes*

Renowned educator and activist Marva Collins once said,

*"Success doesn't come to you. You go to it."*

Too many people have tainted, shortsighted or misguided expectations about success. For one thing success is only the *big picture.* You haven't really topped out until you've totally finished the challenge.

And yet, think about how sports teams win championships or individual athletes obtain their trophies. They wind their way through a series of matches, playoffs or qualifications. They have more winning to do each time, but celebrate varying levels of victory along the way. Baseball players break out the champagne after they've won the division or the conference title and yet the *World Series* is still to come.

There's very powerful potential for results when we *regularly celebrate our progress* as it happens. We can find fulfillment in the tiniest of results and they are usually worth cheering about. The more triumphs we embrace the greater our motivation will be to *never quit climbing.*

We might applaud the accomplishment of one small step forward: a little money saved, a few steps in rehab, two people talking for the first time in a long time, the end of an enjoyable procedure, getting through the first days of a new, but difficult job. Sometimes we aren't in a very good frame of mind when tackling our mountain, making it hard to be optimistic or celebratory.

We might want to ask a couple of our closest encouragers to remind us of some positives or steps forward they've recently seen on our journey. Our overall festivities may be scaled back but that's okay. Celebrate anyway.

I remember being on a challenging hike in Colorado where it seemed like every three steps forward led to two slipping backwards because of the tons of shale that covered our final push to the top. A number of other dads and myself had each taken one of our young teens on the trip.

Working through an adventure company we were accompanied by several stellar guides. These young guys were also big-time skiers and snowboarders in winter so our hike wasn't that hard for them even though they were carrying the heaviest loads.

However, I'll never forget their encouraging words to us every time we made a little progress. It was hard for us to see much headway through our pain but they knew we were getting somewhere. Their comments served as fresh oxygen refilling our emotional lungs.

So, celebrate movement wherever and whenever you can. Like graffiti on a subway car, progress spawns more progress. Look for affirmations on every part of the trail. They are there if you'll keep your eyes open!

*Prepare For False Summits*

While I've warned you several times not to look at the summit, I have to admit that once I get near the top, I can't help but peek (excuse the pun – it's a sickness, really). And frankly, if you're reaching the high point of your mountain look all you want.

However, remember that many mountains have *false summits*. You'll see an outcropping or expanse of rock that looks as though you can't go any further only to discover the hard way that the true summit is still several thousand feet beyond.

If you want a powerful way to kill your motivation on a mountain, get fooled by a false summit. It will take your breath and motivation away in a heartbeat. The mind has a way of storing up enough energy and motivation to accompany our realistic, yet challenging goals.

But when asked to go farther than programmed we can suddenly exhaust the energy needed to finish.

I was part of an East Coast bike trip with high school students years ago. I knew on a particular day our mileage goal was going to be in the 125-130 range but I prepared mentally for it. Along with our riding group, I paced myself and helped our team knock off the miles during a long, hot day.

However, about twenty minutes out one of our leaders came by in the equipment truck and told us we were going to have to add another fifteen or twenty miles on to our total. I was furious! For one thing we should have been told sooner about a last minute change like this.

I yelled at the leader (who happened to be my friend and roommate) driving the truck and showing very little kindness in my response. I told him in quite colorful terms what he could do with my bike, the truck and everything else within a hundred feet. I later apologized and we're still friends.

You see this false summit of sorts was close to a game-ender for us. We did make it, totaling over 150 miles for the day, but that last minute addition was nearly disastrous.

I mentioned in *Chapter 7* that Tim and I also tackled *Mt. Elbert*, a central Colorado mountain and the highest in the state. Remember, how cold it was up there? We'd started early and ascended switchback after switchback for a long time. It was certainly reasonable to think we were nearing the summit.

Moreover, the air was getting colder and there was significant snow left from winter even though we were hiking in July.

Naturally our thoughts turned to summiting. Soon we saw a single climber quickly descending our route. He appeared to be just short of the top! We would meet up with him in just minutes given his quick pace and our continued movement higher.

As he stopped to greet us, we were putting on those warmer layers of clothing. But as we donned our extra sweatshirts and jackets, we shared our eagerness to reach the summit, expecting him to confirm our proximity. Instead, in a wonderful Australian accent he said, *"Sorry mates but you've got a long way yet to the top.'* We had been fooled by a false summit.

You see, life climbers need to scout out where pretend summits might lurk on their trails. For example, we might be anticipating *too quick a recovery*. We think we'll be home, back at work and doing just fine within days or weeks, but months of recuperation are still ahead.

Someone may believe that their financial issues will be resolved because of several easy money schemes only to discover that to be successful will take far longer than they really have.

Our child struggling with an addiction promises that *this time they're going to stay in rehab and get clean.* But we find out that their assurance was just another way to get us off their back and our summit again moved thousands of feet higher.

*A strained relationship* turns a corner and things seem healthy again. We think that perhaps all of our praying, hard work and standing our ground has helped. Things are great for a while, but then the bottom falls out and previous habits, tendencies and responses all reappear.

Like Tim and I encountered on *Mt. Elbert*, false summits can be deceiving, hiding the real summit in ways we can't fix. However, if we know they're a potential problem we can think about asking the experts and caregivers on our team– pastors, counselors, other advisors, medical personnel, friends, etc. – what we might stay alert for that could lead to false hope.

Recognizing a false summit before we encounter it can save us significant angst and leave a little more in our tank to finish the climb. It we know a summit mirage might be ahead, we'll be less likely to get our hopes up and want to quit when it's not really there.

## YOUR NEXT STEP?

Take some time before reading the next chapters to determine what's the logical next part of your climb. What constitutes the upcoming switchback or pitch? Perhaps you already know and just need to affirm it.

Or maybe you've been confused and distracted, not focused on what needs your attention and intentions right now. Hone in on *only* the next thing. Take a deep breath and let go of the rest of your mountain for now.

Take a couple of short steps to enjoy some early success and clarify your direction even more. Pray for wisdom, do more research if needed, talk with your spouse, mentor or counselor about it, nothing more.

Write down what you need to keep giving priority to NOW. Then go back through this chapter and make sure you're following the principles discussed that will help you stay centered until you complete this phase. I guarantee that your anxiety level will drop, you'll sleep better and experience more peace as you continue your climb.

You'll enjoy special sights and experiences along the way, even when the path is more extreme than usual. You'll feel like you're getting somewhere and you will be! Just be sure that you *never quit climbing.*

*Things To Think About in Chapter 8*

Write out exactly what needs to be accomplished on the next part of your climb.

What will be your reward for reaching that level?

Who else do you have or need as an advisor to keep you focused on the *here and now*?

Celebrate with someone close to you a recent success on your journey or your prelude to starting.

# CHAPTER 9: KEY TWO: LIVE IN EACH MOMENT

*"Live your life each day as you would climb a mountain. An occasional glance toward the summit keeps the goal in mind, but many beautiful scenes are to be observed from each new vantage point."*
***Harold B. Melchart***

There is a relentless section of *Long's Peak* that I spoke about earlier called *The Trough*. Experienced hikers and hardened climbers don't sweat it much but we average mountaineers find it demanding. It's a snow-enhanced boulder climb that gradually gets tougher because of its steepness and location approaching fourteen thousand feet.

But it was also here that Tim and I received much needed water from those young guys coming down.

We obviously hadn't planned carefully enough. Nevertheless, their surprising kindness was a small, powerful and impactful highlight that we never forgot. So, let me say right from the start of this principle's discussion:

*It's easy to overlook the little things when the climb is hard.*

Another seemingly insignificant view occurred in the still waters of the Arkansas River. Our rafting group rounded a bend in the river to hear the guide passionately whisper to us to look at on a nearby cliff. There we saw four beautiful mountain goats (which explained the whispering) gazing down on us as though they had no care in the world. Our guide went on to explain what a rare sight this was. *It's easy to overlook the little things.*

I remember most of our homemade lunches eaten in some of the most spectacular mountain spots in the world. The meals themselves weren't that great but the views made them worth millions as far as we were concerned.

In more recent years, after topping out on several summits with each of my kids, I finally did a 14er with the two of them together! I remember getting all choked up as we began our hike just knowing I was climbing with them at the same time!

Did you notice that these examples (and there are hundreds more) didn't usually occur on top of the mountain? They were relished along the way, in a singular moment long before the final trek to the summit.

We mustn't miss or overlook the extraordinary and equally powerful memories made in small, but often unnoticed moments of our journey. They may not be much when placed against larger, more important outcomes or memories.

Nonetheless, they matter big time and in fact can add as much to our overall experience as reaching our final goal. Unfortunately, we can encounter all sorts of reasons or distractions to incredible part-way moments and pass them by.

We're of course naturally focused on our summit, the big reason for the climb, but we'll sacrifice much if we don't embrace these potential moments up and down our mountain.

## WHY WE MIGHT OVERLOOK THE LITTLE THINGS

*Tunnel vision about the summit.*

I've already discussed this problem in the last chapter but it bears some expanded perspective. Remember: *It's very hard to climb a mountain focused on the top.* It's simply too big, too overwhelming, too hard. And yet when we're at the beginning of our journey, when the shock of bad news still echoes in our ears, it's easy to obsess on the final goal.

That's why if you're still looking too far ahead, go back and re-read the last couple of chapters and/or review the questions that follow. This short interlude will help you evaluate your current status. You may need to admit that you haven't figured out your next steps and aren't focused on the current portion of the trail.

As you reduce the amount you're concerned with now, you'll have better eyesight to see little things that are part of each section of trail. (More on that below in, "*Things not to miss.*")

*Painkilling.*

I love Novocain. Okay, I love what it does, not the injections. Ugh. Do you ever get used to a person coming at your mouth holding a needle the size of a pencil? But the reason I value Novocain is that the soreness I would have experienced due to the dentist fixing a cavity, root or other dental problem is eliminated. And who wants more pain in their life, right?

However, when we're under the influence of painkillers, we rarely think wisely or logically. After getting Novocain you can't talk, eat or spit correctly until it wears off. Painkillers, though helpful, tend to limit normal functioning and thinking.

Other non-medical anesthetics do the same. In fact, painkillers are really all about us. They numb our hurt for a while so we can keep avoiding pain rather than heal. When people are approaching or suffering a potentially hurtful life experience, they usually turn to their personal choice of drug, their version of Novocain. Most of us know the usual ones: *alcohol, illicit sex, spending, gambling, work, even religion.*

Some of our addictive behaviors, our pain-reduction strategies, don't involve illegal or socially unacceptable behaviors either. We can become addicted to hobbies, church, volunteer work, being nice, hanging around other people and serving others all for the purpose of avoiding discomfort.

When addicted, however, we don't live in the moment, act alive, feel pain, pressure or other necessary difficult emotions we may need to get to the top of our mountain. We instead *demand* to be pain-free. We don't want to hurt or be uncomfortable anymore.

Before going on to the next chapter and to get the significance of this caution, take some time to identify your current painkillers and determine what you could do to let go of them. Which ones do you need to lay aside so you can start or finish your climb? If you need help exploring their power in your life right now, talk to a counselor, coach, mentor or friend.

*Going too fast.*

I am a wannabe pilot. I'm probably too old to ever gain that status now, but flying fascinates me. I'm still like a little kid on most commercial flights.

I ask my pilot friends or anyone else who understands aeronautics all sorts of questions and rarely miss watching a landing or departing plane at the airport near where we live.

But there's something about flying that you give up as opposed to driving or walking. You miss a lot along the way. You don't get to see or engage interesting people, places and things that dot the roads below.

I remember as a kid when we would drive hundreds of miles each day on vacation. We would take breaks for picnics, pastries, trains and fascinating little towns. That doesn't happen as much today when we fly at 35,000 feet or drive seventy-five mph on the interstate.

There's nothing wrong of course with speed and convenience but on a mountain a more leisurely, observant pace is better. Slow down.

Don't make reaching the top quickly your main objective. Mountain climbing will always require a major slowdown and reevaluation of your schedule and priorities. You can't overcome a major life predicament and maintain your regular, hectic, fast-paced schedule!

## THINGS NOT TO MISS!

*Gratitude.*

Famous preacher, Charles Spurgeon, once said,

> *"It's not how much we have but how much we enjoy that makes happiness."*

Nothing could be truer on a climb. There will always be hard sections, parts of our journey that are brutal and appear impossible.

But remember, there are usually moments, experiences or incredible sights to relish on the way up if we'll look for them. They might include stopping to savor the sheer beauty of where you're standing. Climbing a 13er recently, a friend and I were able to watch the sunrise over the mountains to the east as we stood quietly just above tree line.

It was as though we were seeing an artist's painting produced right before our very eyes. I remember saying to myself, *"Lord, thank you for this moment, one that so few people get to have."* I thought of how privileged I was to have the legs and breath to walk to that spot even though the pains in my body were already intense. Thankfulness gave those discomforts a reprieve as my gratitude for the moment took over.

Perhaps you're facing a physical mountain of cancer. You can still give thanks for the benefits you yet enjoy, a new person you're getting to know or the fact that your situation isn't as hard as someone else's.

Maybe you've been able to regularly encourage one other person *because* of your challenges. You only met them as a result of your unwelcomed climb.

Be thankful for that encounter which would have probably eluded your healthy self.

Some of our mountains will lead us to support groups, rehab centers, hospitals, even funeral homes where we'll connect with others for a few minutes or to start a longer relationship that we would have never had.

One of our favorite experiences on mountain hikes has been seeing wildlife up close and personal. Granted there are some animals you don't want to encounter (i.e. grizzlies, mountains lions, an upset moose), but most of the others are pretty tame if left alone. To see them in the wild, however, borders on a spiritual experience.

Their beauty, size, coloring and demeanor are something very different in a forest or above tree line than in a zoo. We've been so blessed and thankful to observe many of these wonders of creation living in their natural surroundings.

Those spontaneous moments are worth noting, journaling and remembering. But to do so we must take time to let the moments sink in. We can be thankful for similar unexpected interactions and sights during our personal climbs.

Appreciate anything that stands out even in the worst of times. You may have to look for it some of the time and train your eyes to look for those special moments. It will probably encourage you more than you can know. And I'll add some thoughts on this in the next chapter, too.

*The People.*

A few years back I did some rideshare driving in my city to earn a little extra money and get out of the office. I only drove part-time but the work was at times discouraging and tedious, in part because I didn't earn a lot per hour. There were many minutes, even hours, sitting around waiting for the next ride.

Nonetheless, I met a whole new set of people that I would never have encountered without that job. I was especially touched by the ones I was able to help, encourage and inspire through casual conversations. Many of them were climbing their own mountains and needed someone to listen, understand and inspire them to keep going, to *never quit climbing.*

Two young, very interesting ladies got in my backseat one afternoon having ordered a ride to take them home. I picked them up in a somewhat sketchy part of town, but I was used to that. Nevertheless, they'd only been in my car for a minute or two when I was fairly sure that this would be the ride from Hell.

Their expletive-laced conversation and questions centered around sex, how many unplanned places they needed to stop at and a host of other inappropriate comments I tried to ignore. Nonetheless, I did my best to be flexible while wishing the ride would end soon.

Near the end of our magical mystery tour, we stopped at one of their homes so one of the young ladies could give money to her mom. She was actually in the house for five minutes or more when the other young woman without initiation opened up to me.

She began to tell me her story of incarceration, addiction and the removal of a young child from her life. She was doing everything she could to get the child back, paying her bills and obeying the court but no one seemed to be listening or giving her a break.

Apparently, in her mind I was.

Soon she was sobbing in the back seat of the car. I couldn't solve her problem but I was able to help her consider getting her life back by walking up one part of the trail at a time. Sound familiar? I told her she was on the right track.

I gave her one of the wristbands I carry with me. It says, *Never Quit Climbing* on one section and *The View From The Top Is Worth It!* on the other half. With tears flowing down her cheeks she vowed to never take it off. She probably did but she obviously needed to hear that message.

In the middle of my own climbing, I met a person who I was able to nudge, encourage and inspire to keep going. Every time that happens my motivation to encounter more people like her returns even if it means some discomfort, weariness and time that I'd rather be at home.

When we stop and assist someone else, we help ourselves. We add more bounce to our step and air to our lungs because we've taken the attention off us and directed it towards others.

While hiking, we've met people from other countries, those with incredible stories, some from our home state or needy individuals who desired our listening ears. Who knows who you might meet because you were climbing a personal mountain that you wish you'd never faced?

Remember the creation story of the Bible from our earlier discussion? God said to Adam that it wasn't good for him to be alone? Don't forget that's still true today. We're better when someone else is with us. They might be better as well because we showed up.

This ancient wisdom from the Bible is still so and worth remembering:

*"Two are better than one, because they have a good return for their labor: If either of them falls down, one can help the other up. But pity anyone who falls and has no one to help them up."* (4:9-10)

While scaling your mountain anticipate and enjoy the people that you meet. Other people bring strength, purpose, encouragement and new focus to your life and to your climb.

*Small miracles.*

I would guess that those of you reading this book have a variety of opinions on what constitutes a miracle. Some would suggest that most events in life could be termed miracles. Others might argue that a miracle has to be something that doesn't occur in the normal scheme of things, is supernatural and couldn't be manufactured or manipulated by humans.

There's probably some truth in each definition, but my point here does not require a hard and fast underpinning. I put this concept in the list because there are miracle-like moments we've observed in big mountains, both the natural and personal kind, that don't fit any other obvious categories. They too can be missed if we don't live in the moment. A couple of instances are worth mentioning.

I'll never forget when Tim and I climbed *Mount of The Holy Cross*. We had gotten lost and couldn't find the trail back down. At one point we had to backtrack through deep snow only to see a storm headed our way. Upon scampering to a safer area and not worrying about where we would end up, we took what we deemed to be a different trail. We just wanted to get out of there and below the storm.

The miracle occurred when twenty or thirty minutes later we found ourselves on our original trail just further down the mountain. For us that seemed miraculous. We definitely needed something supernatural.

Remember when my daughter and I were near the summit on *San Luis Peak* and a lightning bolt went across the top after we prayed? Coincidence? Maybe. But that felt like something beyond the normal too. Events, things we couldn't explain, have encouraged us and affirmed that a heavenly power was part of our journey too.

Those sorts of miracles show up on personal ascents, even during tragedies, challenges, trials and tribulations that loom in front of us. And we must see them as more than mere coincidences.

We need to watch for them, recognize them and let these potent moments give us extra strength to climb again, even if they mean we must descend for now.

You may recall my describing when Jackie's surgeon told her before her surgery that he wouldn't know if she would have a permanent bag on her side or not until he operated. If the bag was on one side when he finished, she would have it forever. If left on the other side, it was temporary.

The answer would be found in the margin he had when reattaching things following the procedure. There was very little room for error. The good news was that the bag ended up being temporary. She got the best answer! Our celebration was far from the summit, but it became one of several miracles that provided us with greater resolve to finish the climb.

We celebrated that miraculous moment and our hopes for eventually planting a flag on top of our cancer peak rose dramatically!

Miracles don't have to be gigantic to provide big results. A miracle might involve an estranged spouse or other relative finally making contact. A miracle could include a prodigal coming back to church. There are moments on every path where unusual phenomena manifest themselves and empower us to take on one more switchback.

You need to marvel at a forgotten bonus or honorarium that shows up just when needed. It could be a note from a friend who was thinking of you six months after you lost the love of your life. Helen Keller said,

> *"When we do the best that we can, we never know what miracle is wrought in our life, or in the life of another."*

Miracles often show up when we need them, whether they are defined by everyone as miraculous or not. Don't wait for the summit to experience a life-giving, energy enhancing wonder on your way to the top.

*Progress*

We have rarely climbed to higher locations and not seen the distance we'd already come. When fighting altitude our progress always feels slow and as though we're making little headway. But when we stop to peek over our shoulder or descend from the top we are amazed at how much we did cover. We need to periodically review our progress

Talking about past performance or success isn't being inappropriately proud. Old time baseballer Dizzy Dean once said,

"*It ain't braggin' if you can do it!*"

I'm referring to using the truth for our benefit. It highlights the fact that we have not been paralyzed, that we faced a huge challenge and with God's help and the aid of others made it this far. Little can motivate more to finish than that.

Unfortunately, some people have a natural bent to be unsatisfied with anything except the finish. It's the old glass half empty/half full dilemma. Looking at our progress keeps our eyes on the half full perspective.

The point is to take advantage of as many positives as you can all along the trail. Live in the moments, every moment of your journey. Notice I said *live* in the moments. That means to stay human, real and very much alive. You still have purpose, potential and possibilities to live out even when your trail is steep and you've not arrived.

Some of you, however, may be in a sense dying more than living. You've given up and feel you have nothing else to offer until you're over your terrible dilemma. Stop thinking that way! Don't believe the lie. Take on the next part of the trail, but while you're at it keep your eyes open.

Get your eyes off of you for a while. Help someone else. Look for miracles. Live now, in the present. There's much to see and enjoy before you ever reach the top!

*Things to Think About In Chapter 9*

How do you live in the moment in your everyday life? (Or consider how you avoid living in the moment).

If you're currently climbing a personal mountain, discuss a time when you actually did live in the moment and enjoyed it.

Is there something this chapter stirred up that you could do now to live more in the moment of climbing your mountain?

Who are people who you might connect with more in the moment?

Work, home, school, your neighborhood? How could you initiate an in the moment connection there?

# CHAPTER 10: KEY THREE: MONITOR YOUR HEART

*"You change your life by changing your heart."*
***Max Lucado***

On a summer trip to Colorado some years ago, our daughter Amy became dehydrated requiring medical attention in a Vail hospital. Because it was off-season for skiers there were very few people in the Emergency Room that night. Thankfully we were soon told Amy would be fine.

However, as we were waiting for her treatment to finish, I began chatting with one of the nurses. We discussed a variety of topics including my implying that the facility was probably much busier in winter.

I surmised that they must deal with a host of fractures, sprains and breaks during the skiing season. The nurse agreed but responded that they actually encountered more heart problems than orthopedic ones. She explained that people from lower elevations typically fly to Colorado, drive an hour or two to the ski area and as quickly as possible take the chairlift or gondola up to ten thousand feet or more.

Then they start skiing at an elevation they're not accustomed to. As a result, many end up in the emergency room needing treatment for both heart and breathing issues. These eager skiers unfortunately ignored the realities and potential dangers of the thinner air.

The moral of the story: *Heart problems are a regular occurrence in the mountains.*

That's why it's essential to discuss several *heart* concerns that can arise when we scale personal mountains. A weak heart at high elevation can be deadly. A heart out of rhythm above tree line may not kill you but can sure impede your resolve to finish.

The last thing you want in the mountains is a heart attack. Getting to a heart-stricken climber on a peak or cliff is one of the toughest rescue challenges emergency personnel face. In the same way it's extremely hard to repair emotional heart issues once a personal climb s tarts.

Being aware of these potential problems can help us prepare our inner self well before we take our first step beyond the trailhead of our personal journey.

## COMMON *HEART* AILMENTS

*Entitlement syndrome.*

The challenges of life have a way of pulling us inward making us defensive and protective rather than interactive and concerned about others.

Of course, as we encounter big-time problems, we need to pay attention to what's going on inside. It's important that our emotional tanks stay filled, our energy remains high and our mind thinks clearly. We need to strive for balance and not try to accomplish too much too soon.

But many of those facing a significant climb can begin to think that life must now be all about them. They suddenly feel *entitled* to the *best, first and fastest.* They picture everyone else's world stopping or adjusting so that they can always have what they need or want.

They soon find out though that the world isn't braking for them in spite of the seriousness of their predicament. And when it doesn't, they can become bitter, angry or depressed instead of active, intentional and involved.

The idea of serving, caring for and engaging other people is often light years away from their mind, actions and lifestyle. Life is now all about their climb while they try to get every advantage, new procedure, treatment, professional resource, top expert or bit of research that will take them to their goal.

*"It is easy, when you are young, to believe that what you desire is no less than what you deserve, to assume that if you want something badly enough, it is your God-given right to have it."*
*Climber, author Jon Krakauer*

The author of that quote was part of the 1996 disaster on Everest, hiking with one of the two American teams as both an expert high-altitude mountaineer and reporter. Writer of the follow-up book *Into Thin Air,* Mr. Krakauer experienced firsthand the friendly fire of several climbers who thought that getting to the summit was all about them.

They so wanted to summit *Everest.* And they did. They believed they were entitled to make it. Tragically, many of them died as a result. In reality, we must realize everything we have including life itself is a gift not an entitlement program.

*Pride comes before a fall* says the book of Proverbs.

Everything we have is on loan so to speak. Consequently, we're a fool to demand and expect we still don't have what we at first enjoyed. Nonetheless, the anxiety and pressures of our challenge can push us to do just that.

Years ago, I met a man had done house sitting for some friends getting to live in their $600,000 home. He was going to watch the residence for a total of six months. It was an expensive place, especially a couple of decades ago, and its amenities matched the price.

As he neared the end of his stay he was often asked if he was going to miss living there once he returned to his modest home. My acquaintance's reply was simple but profound. *"Yes, I'll miss it. But it's easier to leave it behind when it doesn't belong to you."*

Entitled people have trouble letting go of what they believe belongs to them. Far fewer people would live entitled lives if they just understood that things aren't theirs in the first place.

Some expect extra attention and importance *because* of the mountain they've encountered. They want others to understand that their condition keeps them from acting responsibly or giving anything up right now. *"Don't you know what I'm going through?"* they plead.

And certainly, we will all have needs and face times of testing long after our ascent and descent are over. I've been sore for weeks after climbing a high peak. To this day Jackie has minor symptoms needing ongoing medical attention on a regular basis.

But those lingering issues are no excuse for life during or after our sojourn to become solely about us.

One problem is that when we focus on ourselves and require the best of everything, we drain energy and strength from our reserves. Conversely, courage, joy and greater resolve will grow the more we engage with and serve others during our own hardships.

*"When we give cheerfully and accept gratefully, everyone is blessed."*
*Maya Angeloou*

As we share our stories, ideas, humor, wins, losses, expertise, and encouragement we remain more grounded, future–focused and fulfilled. In fact, one of the ways to lower one's entitlement quotient is to avoid the next heart problem.

*"Life isn't about getting and having, it's about giving and being."*
*Kevin* Kruse

*Pride*

I am very thankful to have summited the peaks I have. They weren't easy and required a major amount of time, money and physical energy. I realize that my determination and perseverance were also a significant part of my success.

That's what we might call *good pride.* The delightful pleasure that accompanies a job well done, a major accomplishment, a new initiative managed or a high mountain climbed is rarely toxic or wrong. This brand of satisfaction motivates rather than paralyzes.

But selfish pride, arrogance and cockiness have no place on a mountain. Mountains are always bigger than we are. Their silent power remains ready at a moment's notice to unleash a fierce retort that our simple strength will never match. If we're in the way, our lives can be over. It's always better to give nature the respect and caution it's due.

The same is true of our personal mountains. While physical harm caused by pride is unlikely, other dangers lurk when we get cocky. Pride that exalts ourselves leads to foolhardiness, relational risk and other poor decisions. Smugness about our progress or success makes us a noisy bother or the instigator of shame and hurt towards those who've not reached similar successes to ours.

Pride saps our gratitude toward those who have sacrificed to help us. If we're people of faith, our cockiness steals praise from God, our guide, strength and provider.

If pride has taken too lofty a place on your journey then you might begin by talking to a few people and asking forgiveness for your self-centeredness.

As I quoted earlier, Proverbs in the Old Testament says, "*Pride comes before a fall,*" so push your ego aside and start focusing on others.

Admit in your apologies that you said things in the heat of the moment or because you were excited about your progress but went too far. Pride will always tempt but thankfully we don't have to give in to it.

*A lack of gratitude.*

In the last chapter I spoke of the importance of being thankful on the way up your mountain as you live each moment. It's very difficult when facing perhaps the biggest obstacle of your life to find anything to be thankful for. It's easier to complain, blame God or others while looking for new ways to dull your hurt.

It's vital then to keep checking your gratitude barometer all along the way, particularly during the hardest times. I'm certainly not suggesting that we be thankful for the trial we're facing. But a tiny little verse in the New Testament simply and wisely says, *"Give thanks in all circumstances."*

The operative word here is, "*In*." I am suggesting that a healthy heart compels us to remain thankful *IN* our circumstances even when they're hard to endure.

Being thankful during a trial allows us to say, *"In spite of my difficulties, I have much to be grateful for."* Gratitude has a way of bringing balance and perspective to the weight and gravity of our problems.

*Be thankful that your situation isn't worse.* There's always someone who has life harder than we do. Sometimes on our journey we need to notice who a few of those people are.

Often, they are sitting near us, live across the street or attend the same church. Seeing their struggle can help us whine less and say thank you more for what we still enjoy that perhaps others don't.

We can be thankful that we live today and not fifty years ago or more. New medicines, changing technology, more informed ideas and myriad other inventions in medicine, finance and psychology were not around just a few decades ago. We're blessed.

My dad had cataracts back in the 80's and 90's. Unfortunately, he contracted them prior to the advances we have today and consequently wore big, thick glasses for a while and spent weeks recuperating and adjusting.

Jackie and I are so grateful that even when she faced cancer some years ago that surgical techniques had advanced significantly. Her surgeon could perform the amazing work he did which spared her much more discomfort and challenge.

Fifty years ago, many more died from common maladies. Decades ago, there weren't the jobs, income and online opportunities to better oneself that we enjoy today. There weren't as many caring professionals and competent church leaders available to help hurting people. We can be filled with gratitude for those benefits!

*Be thankful for the progress you've already made.* I spoke of this earlier but let me say it one more time. Stop and enjoy the current scenery now and then. You're missing some of the best views if your eyes are always staring at your feet. Don't forget to look back and see how far you've come.

Ask someone else to give you their perspective too because sometimes we need a person outside of our sphere of influence to encourage us. They see positive things we don't.

*Be thankful for the special people in your life.* Periodically, it might be therapeutic to make a list of individuals or families who have been key players on your journey. Take some time to appreciate each one of these individuals: *medical people, family, advisors, legal counsel, friends, fellow strugglers, helpers, cooks* to name a few.

Chances are someone has or will come along who inspires you beyond words and gives you the will to live, succeed and overcome again.

*"What separates privilege from entitlement is gratitude."*
*Brene Brown*

*Risk aversion*

What do all the following have in common? Riding a bike, taking out a loan, learning to drive, ice skating, asking someone special out on a date?

They were all risky the first time we did them. In fact, some risk probably followed and remained for a while after our initial venture. Though avid bike rider who's covered over seven thousand miles on a two-wheeler, a number of years ago I fell turning a sharp corner. I got all skinned up just a few days after moving into our new home in Illinois.

Risk is a fact of life and something we can't avoid even if we stay holed up in our home on the couch watching television. Helen Keller once said,

*"Security is mostly a superstition. Life is either a daring adventure or nothing."* (*Let Us Have Faith*)

There's no fancy phobia name for the fear of risk, but atychiphobia, the fear of failure, may be close. Many times we won't try something new because we're terrified that we might fail. *What if I don't reach the summit? What if I make a mistake and blow my chance to reach the top?*

But people who fear risk won't succeed at much of anything. The potential hazards are too dangerous in their minds. Yet everything we do essentially has some gambles attached to it. The key is knowing the difference between taking a risk and being foolish.

Foolhardiness implies that we take chances without having thought through our potential for success, the level of our skills and the resources we have to pull it off.

For me to try one of free climber Alex Honnold's high difficulty climbs would be foolhardy. I'm not strong enough, skilled enough or young enough.

However, if Alex were kind enough to help me attempt a simpler route, even with multiple ropes and other protection, there would still be risk involved. It's possible that the equipment could break, rocks come loose or bad weather shows up. But risk isn't a logical reason to avoid climbing.

Getting our heart right about danger means that we have learned to prepare well and to embrace faith that our accumulated wisdom will provide us the safety and protection we need.

*Being Untouchable*

You have probably noticed that several of these heart issues focus on a *self-focused life* rather than an *other–centered* one. And when the attention all turns our direction, we will begin to distance ourselves from people around us.

We'll go out less, skip more social gatherings, avoid church or other people–centric activities. We won't talk about ourselves or desire to know much about others' problems either. We'll avoid answering most phone calls and quit group settings we may have enjoyed in the past.

Instead of engaging in a controlled, manageable ascent of our *Everest, o*ur personal mountain may begin to control us! We won't think about much else and would rather people stay out of our lives until we're finished.

People may reach out to us but we may push them away. We have little time or energy for them because we think we need it all for our predicament. A major way to monitor your heart on this one is to regularly examine your schedule and connection quotient.

Have you given up on people? When's the last time you went out anywhere or enjoyed a special activity with someone other than you or your spouse?

*A don't–call-me perspective*

Do you remember the people I mentioned in an earlier chapter who came alongside us during Jackie's cancer? One in particular was Ann who took Jackie to treatments even though she had lung cancer herself.

It's important to monitor your heart by evaluating your interest in others while you climb your own *Denali*. Have you decided that your struggle is too hard to take time to care for others? Have you looked the other way even though someone could use your help?

Is "*Don't call me,*" the sign on your forehead?

You see, a healthy heart prompts climbers to assist someone else even though their own journey isn't finished. Healthy hearts build up those around them and share their time, insights and experiences. As I've said a number of times, they know that being thoughtful towards others is actually a way to care for oneself.

So, how's your heart? Are you monitoring it? *"Above all else, guard your heart, for it is the wellspring of life." Proverbs 4:24*

Listen to those wise words on this one. Be smart. Don't have a heart attack. Monitor your attitudes, thinking and resultant actions. *A good attitude will always get you more altitude!*

## THINGS TO THINK ABOUT IN CHAPTER 10

What is my number one heart issue from the list in this chapter or elsewhere?

What do I need to do or work on to keep that issue from recurring and/or growing?

Who could be my accountability partner to help me see heart problems before they develop further?

What else should I consider doing to guard my heart better?

# CHAPTER 11: ENJOYING THE SUMMIT/ DESCENDING

*"It is not the mountain we conquer, but ourselves."*
*Sir Edmund Hillary*

*Long's Peak* was my first triumph with a fourteen-thousand-foot peak, the initial one of nine so far. Seven plus hours and eight miles after leaving the trailhead Tim and I proudly stood together on top.

As you now know it was the culmination of thousands of steps including a steep, switchback-laden path, countless huge boulders, narrow ledges, a relentless trough of climbers' trail in summer snow and a final gut checking home stretch to 14,255 feet. More significantly it was the finale of a dream fulfilled.

We were elated and exhausted. The weather on top was perfect. No sneaky mountain storms lurked nearby threatening to shorten our stay or kill us. Our bodies ached (mine more than his) even as we hugged and high-fived, thankful for our accomplishment that even included that extra hiker.

We needed a few minutes to catch our breath, remove our packs and finally sit down. Longing to relish the moment, we began to gaze at the view all around us as though we could see forever. Was this the top of the world?

The city of Denver provided a visual gateway to the vast Midwestern plains to the east. Dozens of other 14ers, part of the fifty plus in Colorado, were stunningly prominent to the west. We could only dream of tackling more in the coming years.

It's hard to describe the range of emotions that welled up during our short stay there. In fact it was surprisingly difficult for me at first to describe my strongest feeling in those moments.

The hardships during our eight-mile ascent faded in the presence of newly found elation. But there was something else that I strongly sensed as we stepped onto the summit. I remember wondering if it was just a high level of happiness, perhaps a deeper peace about reaching a decades old goal.

Several years prior I had begun a personal study of a word that had always intrigued me. It's a powerful term, one I'd used many times, but suspected its core was deeper and richer than I'd discovered up to that point.

It shows up quite often in the Bible but in varied contexts.

The word? *JOY*. This common, yet infrequently spoken term is nonetheless a rich one. It's a lump-in-the-throat passion that resides and flourishes in the crevasses of our souls and yet often bursts onto the scene of our relationships and other special moments without warning.

And yet it is often relegated to *holiday-only* status. *Joy to the world, the Lord is come* is sung by many each Christmas. Fewer and fewer women still own it as their name, however. Can you think of a contemporary, secular song that contains the word *joy*? I doubt it.

*Joy* only has three letters but it's miles deep. We've probably experienced it at times we didn't know if was there.

Don't parents feel joy when they hold their newborn? Isn't it a cause for joy seeing a transformed, changed, renewed life? If we saw a miracle happen wouldn't that move us to joy?

Joy accompanies healings of diseases, love in relationships, designs in nature and the intricacies of the human body. There are thousands of moments that bring us joy, right?

Are you starting to see a common thread here? There is something starkly inherent in every genuinely joyful moment.

## WHAT IS JOY?

Gary's definition*: Joy is what we feel whenever we experience the grace, mercy, majesty and power of something or Someone bigger than us.*

That's what I experienced on that first ascent and those that followed. Standing at 14,255' of elevation, with only the sound of our voices breaking the silence, having reached a huge goal with one of my own children was a special gift of grace that I didn't deserve. *It brought me joy like I've just described because for me God was powerfully present.*

In my heart, a sense of bigness was very evident that day. Climbing my mountain brought more than happiness. It was joy.

I now boldly assert that we can and must look for joy in the middle of our pain while on our trek to the summit. We can have joy on the journey, in the waiting room, when the bills aren't paid or when we feel like a failure.

Joy can show up in both the best and the worst of times. Joy will be ours in an arid desert or lush garden, while content or at a loss, living in luxury or hardship, exhilarated or exhausted.

Happiness is outward and wonderful in its own right when we find it. However, it is fleeting, dependent upon the responses of others. And if we don't receive the reactions we desire our happiness will depart.

Joy however requires no other human support though we may welcome and relish it when it comes. Humans are capable of bringing us joy of course. When another person is still there with you while you feel unworthy, rejected and unimportant that is also a reason for joy.

When they tell you what you've meant to them or how valuable your relationship is that's a joy moment. That is joy from the *horizontal* in the context of relationship.

But we can't expect any person to be the only source of our joy. If we do, we'll keep demanding more and more that they can't give. For our joy, we must always make Someone bigger the foundation realizing that only that bigger, greater being can be the ultimate and unchanging joy giver.

I remember feeling overwhelmed on top of *Long's* thinking about how few people would sit where Tim and I sat. We remained there maybe forty-five minutes knowing that we would likely never pass that way again. We certainly couldn't re-live that moment.

But it was clearly a *joy moment*, an experiencing of the grace of a Creator, the majesty of His handiwork and the incredible power it took to create it all. Even if you're not a faith person, you would have to be impacted in some way seeing the complexity and size of what's around you.

Eventually we sat down and began to devour our simple lunch. As usual, the peanut butter sandwiches tasted like steak while the extra water from the guys on the way up soothed our parched throats like a clear, cool spring. All that was a welcome addition to our joy!

When you're on your way to your summit, look for something bigger there. Seek it a second time when you reach the top. Don't settle for mere happiness. Soak in rich, powerful, tear-producing joy.

Take time to celebrate the greatness of the world in which you live and revel in the irresistible delights you were given by a loving, powerful, graceful Creator.

Of course if you're not a person of faith, you might respond differently. Whatever your background you can still experience this deeper emotion I'm describing as joy. And perhaps your journey will cause you to consider God's role in that emotion. What can it hurt?

Perhaps you saw Him, felt Him or at least wondered about what He might be doing behind the scenes. Don't miss this opportunity to at least open the door to faith in a God and a world beyond what you can see.

Climbing a mountain, especially a life mountain, is a big deal. It rarely happens casually or void of problems. You reach the top because of a commitment to make it, through the help of supportive people and a trust in the God of the universe who cared enough to walk alongside you.

That's why you can't rush your summit experience. Don't run past the joy. After conquering your personal mountain take time to celebrate, enjoy the greatness of the moment and embrace *joy*.

Gather your fellow travelers together and have a party. They were there for you so let them revel a bit, too. If you're willing thank God for the win. Commit before the group to someday assist others with their climb and find joy in their successes.

I love how the Bible often talks about people dancing, singing, writing poetry, feasting and doing whatever else to celebrate God's grace in giving them a win. We don't do enough of that today but mountain climbing is one of those times when we need to let it all out.

Celebrate the magnitude of your accomplishment by re-calculating how much you've overcome. It you had an addiction to pain pills but took on the challenge of receiving help, weaning off the meds, altering your lifestyle and even thinking differently about your life, value and personhood, applaud it! That's worth shouting about.

But you must also take some time on the summit to consider the potential dangers on your descent. Starting down a steep pitch or rocky trail without preparation can have disastrous consequences.

## GET READY FOR THE TRIP DOWN

My wife and I have learned to appreciate trekking poles. Some people mistake them for modified ski poles but they are actually designed for climbers. They adjust to your size and fold down small enough to fit in a backpack when you don't need them.

But one of their most important functions is to provide balance and support going down. They take pressure off the knees and serve as *handrails* to keep you from stumbling or falling when your legs are extra tired.

In descending a life climb we can also benefit from a figurative set of poles that can steady us on one of the most dangerous parts of scaling a mountain.

It's worth repeating:

> *"Getting to the top is optional, but getting down is mandatory. A lot of people get focused on the summit and forget that."*
> **Ed Viesturs**, *No Shortcuts To The Top*

*Anticipate possible problems.*

Let's return one more time to the tragedy on *Everest* in 1996. Most members of the two American teams actually reached the top. Their excitement must have been exhilarating! I would guess that some had tears in their eyes and a lump in their throats having realized a decades long dream in some cases.

Flags were planted, hugs given and pictures taken. What an amazing time of celebrating it must have been if only minutes long.

Sadly, only a few of them made it back to base camp. Most of the victims died above twenty-four thousand feet as sixteen lost their lives that day.

As I chronicled earlier, the leaders of the two teams didn't hold to their pre-described guidelines for summiting. They pushed the envelope multiplying the potential problems heading down.

The point is that we dare not start down any mountain without revisiting the seriousness of the dangers ahead. We may not be trapped in a storm on *Everest,* but there are similar whiteouts that can cause significant harm even after a hard-fought victory over a major mountain.

Think about it. On a granite peak, the perils climbers face going up are often still there when they return. The difficulties can be worse because of fatigue or the fact that gravity pulls in a different direction, one that can exacerbate a fall. Down climbing, as experts call it, can be just as dangerous as heading up a steep pitch.

You might be saying at this point, *"I understand the potential dangers of descending a real mountain but what's so tough about heading down a personal one?* Let me suggest several important warnings:

*You may lose relationships that were important to you.*

People who have enjoyed assisting you on your climb will realize they are no longer needed to the same extent.

You won't call them as often or want to talk as much about your struggle. They can become angry or very sad because of the distance between you now and feel like you're dropping them as a friend.

They have to grieve the loss of being sorely needed and sometimes won't handle those feelings well. They may walk away from you for good, even tell friends of their dislike for or disappointment with you.

That of course can cut deeply and be dangerous to your mental and emotional well-being if you're not prepared for it. Their response can drain much of the excitement you've built up during your long sojourn and initial celebrations. (I'll add some details on this in the final chapter.)

*You may grieve the loss of your mountain.*

Who would think that getting over a major hurdle would cause anyone to wish they still had it?

You might be thankful at first for the lessening angst, but you can start to miss the tension and busyness. Much of the attention, energy, information gathering, passion, prayer, adrenaline and relationship building that drove you hard to summit can fade as you descend.

What was such an integral part of your life is now becoming a memory. You are now required to live life rather normally and forfeit most of the attention you received for so long. Grief usually results in multiple permutations of denial, anger and sadness, even depression.

You may find yourself experiencing all of those feelings and more as though someone died. But no one passed away. Only your struggle was terminal.

*You may still make old mistakes.*

Remember me discussing when Tim and I were descending Mt. of the Holy Cross? This is the peak where we got off track during our down climb but eventually found our original trail as a storm approached.

In the early going I stepped down from a large boulder to a smaller one causing my weary and weakened ankle to turn hard. Pain shot through my whole body and I limped the rest of the way back to the trailhead. Only tightly-tied, well-made boots plus several doses of painkillers got me back to the car.

Ankles can be injured for numerous reasons but my problem occurred because I was tired. And as soon as my leg couldn't support me my body weight caused it to collapse. The result could have been far worse than the purple-y mess it became later that day.

We face similar weariness after a life climb. Fatigue can cause us to lash out, be short with others, yell at family and friends or demand that people act or respond in certain, atypical ways. We may not turn an ankle but might turn a relationship for the worse.

It's best to think ahead and predict when and how we are most likely to be vulnerable. Call on your mentors and other partners to help think through healthy responses or to be your lookouts for potential accidents for a while. Which leads to . . .

*Commit To Taking Your Time*

Your climb has likely been more of a marathon than a sprint. You didn't run up the mountain. You walked it switchback after switchback, day after day, week after week, and maybe year after year.

In doing so you expended a lot of mental, physical, emotional and spiritual energy.

As we highlighted earlier, during your reverse trip your strength may be depleted and when you're exhausted you're more likely to mess up. Climbers on *Everest* and other peaks are often injured or fall to their deaths on the descent not the upward climb. Their minds are foggier and legs weaker. Every step is a chore and balance can turn dicey.

And at altitudes above 20,000 feet, walking on precipitous slivers of snow and ice next to thousand-foot drops make chances of a catastrophic fall extremely high. The percentages for disaster are also elevated when climbers have limited reserves in their tanks.

For example, we can be weaker during our first few days or weeks after summiting. Remember, we may say things to others that are insensitive and unkind. We can make poor decisions and choices because we don't have the clarity of mind that we'll enjoy again once our reserves have been replenished.

As you begin to live in your post-summit moments, focus hard on not letting relationships fail, managing grief and making wise choices. That process is fostered in part by taking your time. While still basking in the glow of your conquest, *go slowly* as you move ahead. Remember my earlier examples regarding what to avoid.

If you've just reached the downward side of a major illness or disease, don't return too soon to your old way of life until you've regained your strength and adjusted to resultant lifestyle changes.

Get down your mountain. Do it safely. Be patient. Continue to enjoy your progress and the satisfaction of making it.

*Lay aside new summits (for now).*

Nineteenth century Austrian composer Gustav Mahler, apparently an avid hiker, once said,

> *"When I have reached a summit, I leave it with great reluctance, unless it is to reach for another, higher one."*

Of course, there's nothing wrong with success breeding more success. There are more victories that can result from this one. But the time to ponder and plan for another is not while descending your mountain and heading back to the valley. That kind of response has the potential to cause another distraction that can lead to a fall or misstep along the way.

Jackie has talked about how she dreaded much of the nine months leading up to the birth of our kids. There was the morning sickness, her changing body, and the worsening awkwardness. Then after they were born came the extended days of pain following hours of unsuccessful pushing and major surgery (both our kids were born by Caesarean section).

But she also describes how she soon forgot the pain and discomfort of childbirth. It took a while but holding that new little life in her arms was a powerful antidote to the agony and trauma of becoming a mother.

Being able to disregard the distress of both pregnancy and delivery is certainly a blessing. However, even mothers need to remember that their reserves are depleted during those early days.

They must give almost all their attention to a precious, but needy bundle of joy while acknowledging that any extra resources they once had are pretty much gone.

The same will be true during our descent. Our reserve energy wanes or is very limited so this is not the time to be dreaming about going after our next big peak. Save that option for later and a more appropriate time.

Just as our muscles need time to rest when taxed from a workout, our personhood needs a break to reboot and restore. On the way down don't waste the little reserve remaining in your emotional tank by planning your next conquest.

When you're ready to descend, grab your poles, put on your lightened pack but be sure you're ready for the long trip back to everyday life. It will take a while. You must be careful.

Don't forget that on a true mountain hike many if not most of the things you saw on the way up will still be there during your descent. The difference is that you have opportunity to view them from another perspective. The new light directions can change the look of a lake, the size of shadows or the appearance of animals in the distance.

There may be sights you also missed on the ascent because you had your back to them. Now they're right in front of you. Don't overlook these valuable opportunities to make your return trip more interesting, insightful and inspiring.

In the same way, coming off your personal mountain can include new or improved views as well. For example, using your transformed perspective you may have less expectations of people.

You will hopefully have lowered your demand to change them. You will respond in new ways that are no longer destructive, manipulative or demanding.

Certain triggers that were the focus of an addiction may still be active. But this time new strength and insights from your climb can guide you past them. Returning to the trailhead is the healthy and right time to look at the summit. Now instead of having to fear it, you can take pride having conquered it.

Stand on that reality as you head back to sea level. You did make it. You overcame. Be thankful. No one can ever take that away from you as you move forward.

That's what I'll discuss in the final chapter.

*Things To Think About in Chapter 11*

What do you think you will need to worry about most heading down from your climb?

Is going too fast a possible problem for you? What could you think about doing now that would slow you down?

What other summits could be looming that might distract you on your descent?

What have you celebrated or will you want to celebrate on your summit? Are you a *celebration* kind of person? If not, whom might you need in your life that could help you enjoy the moments on top?

# Part IV: What's Next?

# Chapter 12: Returning To Sea Level

*"Everybody wants to reach the peak, but there is no growth on the top of a mountain. It is in the valley that we slog through the lush grass and rich soil, learning and becoming what enables us to summit life's next peak."* ***Andy Andrews***

I vividly remember how my family always finished our mountain getaways. We would head east from a scenic location such as Denver, Banff, The Tetons, Yosemite or wherever. My dad would then challenge us kids to look back and see how long the mountains were visible. Once we told him that they were finally out of sight he would reveal how many miles we had come.

Some years there wasn't a cloud in the sky while other times the visibility was limited. The sight distance to our beloved peaks varied each time. But I do recall a reoccurring, yet profound feeling that always accompanied my dad's trick to keep us entertained for a while.

S*adness*. Each trip I grieved that I wouldn't see the big mountains again for a long time. I knew we were headed back to the flat lands only to soon long for the high country. In the meantime, I would miss the beauty, challenge, smell and even mystery of the high places and desperately wish I were there.

A couple of days after our departure, we would pull into our driveway and everything we had enjoyed out west would feel like a dream. *Did we really climb that mountain? Were we actually walking in snow a few days ago? Will we return soon? Maybe we could just move to the mountains!*

But it wasn't a dream. Instead it was time to live again in our old surroundings. Coming home meant we had to restart life in the valley, at ground zero so to speak, with hopefully our lessons learned and special memories to guide and influence.

*"You climb to reach the summit, but once there, discover that all roads lead down." Stanislaw Lem*

You too will have to face everyday life now and ready for a return to the routine following your summit. However, having overcome your personal mountain, you won't want to live as you did before. The journey has taught you much and imprinted your thinking with life-changing concepts. Things can be different.

But be aware that during your re-entry to home life you can experience discomfort and even awkwardness. It will be like riding a bike, ice skating or driving for the first time. You're doing something new but not comfortable at first.

You wonder what your new *normal* might look like? You will naturally ponder how you can try out your mountain skills in the flat land. If you find yourself unsure where to start once you're back at lower elevation, here are some ideas.

*Reacquaint with the familiar.*

One of the first things families or individuals do when they return from vacation is to open up the house.

They unlock things, re-check what's there, see if anything is missing and re-set the temperature, lights and alarms to reflect that people are present again. We must perform similar reviews returning from our climb.

*Re-visit key relationships.*

As I detailed earlier, sometimes relationships may wane after you get healthier. People don't feel they're needed in your life anymore. And of course that may actually be true. You've overcome your mountain and are starting to function more on your own with renewed strength, courage and transformed thinking.

However, there are also relationships that you want to hold on to or re-start that will require your attention. Thankfully many who helped you and became close will back away willingly. They're mature enough to know that they were only needed for a limited time and will gladly return the relationship to what it was before.

In contrast, there will be others who eagerly jumped in to assist you and were beneficial to your success. Unfortunately, they don't understand or accept that their usefulness and proximity to you must end or at least change.

These people are harder to work with but it will be important that you don't ignore them. They probably won't grasp your backing away but they need to see why you must.

You'll need to be gracious, but firm. Here's a sample response:

> *"Angela, I can't thank you enough for the help you gave me all these months. I couldn't have done it without you and the others who urged me up my mountain. I am going to miss some of those times we just had to talk during the process but I want to encourage you to next share your availability and care with others.*
>
> *One of the things my progress has shown me is that I need to actually cut back on some of the responsibilities and yes, relationships, that I am tempted to take on. I hope you'll understand that and encourage me to live using the new principles I've learned to embrace. I want to stay in touch from time to time but I'm going to have to say no to meeting regularly or coming to your group on a regular basis."*

Other relationships that you did want to continue may have taken a backseat for a while. You didn't have the time, energy or focus to maintain them on your climb. You also know however that you don't want to lose those friends either. They matter, add value to you and help fill your tank. You probably do the same for them.

In those situations, call the person or couple and explain your desire to reconnect. Don't over-commit, but have a first meeting, coffee or phone call and get caught up. Chances are they were hoping you would get back to them and will feel relieved that you reached out. In fact, it's possible that your relationship can actually be healthier than ever!

*Re-assess tempting settings.*

Let me reinforce this idea that I also started earlier. We all have triggers that can cause us to revert to life before our climb. It was a time when we weren't as strong, lacked current resources and responded to difficulties out of habit and fear.

Currently we have new assets and stockpiles to pull from but the circumstances that used to bring us down may still be present. These former attractions may even rear their heads during our descent and catch us off guard once we're back down.

For example, if your mountain were an addiction, you would be wise to identify the places, people and events where that addiction was strongest. *Do you need to avoid some of those places even though you're stronger? Do you need to stay away from certain people who will want to pull you back into that life?*

If you overcame a major health scare or financial crisis, are there things, people or situations that could dramatically set you back?

Have you determined ahead of time (practice in the still water) what you will do if you confront those scenarios now (life in the rough water)? Are you doing the things you must do to live healthier and victoriously from now on?

We don't need to fear temptation if we're prepared for it!

*Strengthen healthy thinking.*

It's likely that within your victory over your mountain, you needed to re-wire faulty thoughts about you and life in general. Friends, spiritual leaders, mentors, counselors and other professionals probably played a role in helping you *renew your mind* or change your thinking. Remember this verse from earlier?

*"Don't be conformed to this world but be transformed by the renewing of your mind." (Romans 12:1)*

That means that your fundamental thinking about where life, hope, purpose and self-esteem come from may have changed or is still in process. You no longer look for those important needs to all be met in people but you're likely still adjusting to letting them go.

You realize now that your worth and value does not have to come from others. Others can reinforce, affirm and remind you of your true source of life but people cannot be the ultimate answer. They will always be fallible and imperfect.

You understand that the now classic movie line from *Jerry Maguire, "You complete me,"* was never true. No one can complete us. No relationship, circumstance, accomplishment, award or amount of anything can fill up our empty spaces. Enjoy them for who they are, find joy in their friendship and encouragement, but let go of them for who you used to demand they be.

Overcoming most mountains and being able to tackle them one switchback at a time requires this key understanding and perspective. Ideally you have already sensed freedom and peace around it.

However, you must also receive regular truth reminders because people and life in general will keep sending opposing messages. We also forget how powerfully individuals and things can tempt us to revert to old thinking.

If we hear a song, truth, poem, etc. over and over, what happens? How did you learn *The Star-Spangled Banner* or *Pledge to the Flag?* You didn't go home one day and memorize either, did you? No, you heard them day after day, game after game, one time after another until they were imprinted on your brain.

We must hear the real truth about ourselves over and over too. Let me suggest a few good options:

Go to church regularly.
Learn more about and study the Bible.
Read great books about where life is truly found.
Join a small group or study.
Meet regularly with a couple of close friends.

*Live Out The Significance of Your Climb*

When you return to lower elevations as you would after a mountain vacation, you can respond several ways. You could live as though the trip was a dream and never happened. With that perspective, life just goes back to the way it was.

Nothing really changes. You may as well not have tackled your mountain in the first place. Your efforts may have a temporary effect but will accomplish little.

A second, healthier response is to treat your victory as incredibly significant, powerful and life–changing. That means that while some of life will be lived as it was before, you will bring a new you to that existence. The differences will become obvious to others but are some practical ways to fortify your changes.

*Talk to people about your climb.*

I've been a pastor, speaker and teacher for most of my adult life so I've literally given hundreds of talks, messages and inspirational speeches. And there is one habit that I've found incredibly helpful prior to addressing a group.

I teach the message out loud at least five or six times. I speak or read it the first time in my office. I may also do that a second time after some revisions. I then go present it in a large room as though the audience is packed with hundreds.

After I do more edits based on my run throughs, I teach it at least a couple of other times in the location where I will give my talk or message.

You know what that does? It seals and cements the concepts, stories, illustrations and general purpose of the talk into my mind and soul. While I still use notes, I find the presentation now flows more naturally because I've already taught it numerous times.

The same happens when we talk to others about our personal mountain experience. Habits and actions begin to transform because we're imprinting them on our hearts and minds every time we talk.

We don't need to tell the whole world. In fact, be cautious about using social media for this. Public posts should be used only to compel interest from people to learn more.

However, we do need to repeatedly share our story with the people closest to us and those most likely to be impacted by the lessons from our journey. In fact, have your radar on to listen for appropriate opportunities to share your story. I often find it helpful to ask people for permission before I just dive in.

As people of faith, Jackie and I pray for *divine appointments* to encourage someone at just the right moment to *never quit climbing.* But the more we tell about our journey, the more concise, clear and helpful our words become. Repetition helps us learn what to say, what works and what does not.

We affirm for anyone who will listen that the view from the top really is worth it!

*Incorporate fundamental changes.*

Life back home also requires that we live out the lessons learned on our climb. Those insights will only become entrenched in us and truly transform if we practice them within the fabric of daily life.

If conquering your mountain requires food and drink adjustments, then make the changes now to help you confidently move forward and avoid more problems. If continued success requires certain habits be instituted every day, then begin as soon as you return home.

Most of the mountains we climb require thought transformation as I discussed in the previous section. However, we can't just understand these new concepts. We must also live them!

Let's say you overcame a financial mountain, worked your way out of debt and got your finances in some semblance of order. That's progress but your long-term financial stability must also reflect fresh thoughts about you.

*I'm an okay person whether rich or not. I sometimes dull my pain through spending and it never ultimately works. I don't need to keep up with anyone. My job is not where my value resides.*

These ideas may or may not represent your struggle or new thinking but you get the idea. Come up with the phrases you need to keep repeating to yourself and have others affirm for you. Then be sure your new actions follow.

That way when it comes to money you actually start spending differently. When you feel good about yourself you no longer go buy something to dull the hurt. You stay out of debt. You spend less and save more. You see the need to develop a budget as you wisely keep track of what you have. Those are all actions that might be a result of your new attitudes about finances.

In fact, it's when you act upon your victory that you find more joy and satisfaction each day. It's how you'll keep the memories of your climb alive and develop meaningful stories to share with others.

With a mentor, counselor, pastor, friend or other influential helper you might revisit some of the critical concepts that you wrestled with on your trek. Review them together and discuss other steps you could take to start implementing them.

Include a follow up and accountability plan to keep your thoughts about yourself healthy and assure that your progress continues. One of the best longer-term strategies is to invest time and energy in a small group as well where you help each other keep climbing and affirm who you are apart from your circumstances.

*Seek Out Someone Else You Can Help*

There will come a time, though not right away, when your new ways of thinking, acting and feeling will be more the norm than the exception. You'll incorporate them naturally into everyday life in the valley.

When you get to that point it will be time to search for another climber who you might mentor and accompany up their mountain. Because you have learned to summit, hike a steep trail to the top and embrace new ways to move forward, you can effectively walk with someone else and help them join the throng of overcomers.

You can redeem your struggle and turn it into a legacy for those who live in fear as you did. You can become the one who walks them toward and through the unknowns that threaten to paralyze them.

Of course, you can't force them to embrace your same passions and results. But you can listen to their stories, share your journey and hope for the same kind of fundamental changes in them.

Has the challenge to *never quit climbing* become more real to you? Are you willing to share your story now, too with others? While you can't take away their mountain, you can help them climb it and do it well.

The important thing to remember is that everyone has a story and their own mountain to climb. They need someone to meet them where they are and inspire them to reach the top.

As one of my professors in grad school used to say, "*People are hurting more deeply than we know.*" In our context we might change his words to, *"Everyone has a mountain they're climbing, big or small."*

You're needed and can do what Jackie and I have been doing. Don't let your walk to the summit, a past one or one yet ahead, go to waste. Look for opportunities to offer what you have learned to others. *The best is yet to come!*

## SO FINALLY . . .

*Before you put this book down*

*Will you commit to take a first or next step*? Remember you have to start somewhere. Include thorough preparation and a meeting or two with a mentor or guide. But please don't wait any longer to begin. The sooner you head up your mountain the better. Don't panic. Just pursue the next thing and do it now.

Confidently begin your step-by-step journey to beat the struggles and challenges that have paralyzed you. Go back and re-read any chapters that may help start out on the right footing.

Others of you at this juncture are part way up your mountain but not sure how to continue and finish well. Your climb so far has been inconsistent and maybe a bit misguided. If so, use what you've read to steer you onto a more productive, careful and thoughtful path to the top and a safe trip back down.

You may be overwhelmed but you don't have to be defeated! *Never quit climbing.* Keep going wherever you are at this point. The good news is that with every step you're closer to the top! Lay aside what has happened in the past, set your eyes on your next waypoint and eat some chocolate!

As Dr. Seuss once wrote, *"Today is your day! Your mountain is waiting, So… get on your way!"*

NEVER QUIT CLIMBING.
THE VIEW FROM THE TOP IS WORTH IT!

## THINGS TO THINK ABOUT IN CHAPTER 12

In one sentence summarize what you learned from this book.

Who comes to mind as a person(s) who you want joining you on your climb?

What are two of the first things you need to do to get better prepared or to continue your climb?

What are some of the key *doors* that you need to open when you finish your climb and return home?

# APPENDIX

## Mountain Climbing Inspiration

*No Shortcuts To The Top,* Ed Viesturs,
*Into Thin Air,* Jon Krakauer
*Banner In The Sky,* James Ramsey Ullman
*Alone On The Wall,* Alex Honnold

## Restoration and The Christian Walk

*Understanding The Wounded Heart,* Marcus Warner
*The Pressure's Off,* Larry Crabb
*Emotionally Healthy Spirituality,* Peter Scazzero
*The Life You've Always Wanted,* John Ortberg
*The Healing Path,* Dan Allender
*You Gotta Keep Dancin',* Tim Hansel

## Overcoming Dysfunction and Wrong Thinking

*Boundaries,* John Townsend & Henry Cloud
*The Healing Path,* Dan Allender
*The Life Model,* Jim Wilder
*Shattered Dreams,* Larry Crabb

## When Bad Things Happen

*Authentic Faith,* Gary Thomas
*The Question That Never Goes Away,* Phil Yancey
*When God Doesn't Make Sense,* James Dobson

# ONE LAST THING

Thanks so much for reading *Never Quit Climbing!* I hope it has been helpful and will ultimately change your life and help you be an overcomer.

However, if you enjoyed NQC would you leave me a review on Amazon.com? Thanks so much.